Greece Travel Guide

Discover the Magic of Ancient History, Stunning Islands and Greece's Timeless Wonders. Pocket Edition

Jason Argyropoulos

© Copyright 2025 by Jason Argyropoulos
All rights reserved

This document is geared towards providing exact and reliable information with regards to the topic and issue covered. The publication is sold with the idea that the publisher is not required to render accounting, officially permitted, or otherwise, qualified services. If advice is necessary, legal or professional, a practiced individual in the profession should be ordered.

From a Declaration of Principles which was accepted and approved equally by a Committee of the American Bar Association and a Committee of Publishers and Associations.

In no way is it legal to reproduce, duplicate, or transmit any part of this document in either electronic means or in printed format. Recording of this publication is strictly prohibited and any storage of this document is not allowed unless with written permission from the publisher. All rights reserved.

The information provided herein is stated to be truthful and consistent, in that any liability, in terms of inattention or otherwise, by any usage or abuse of any policies, processes, or directions contained within is the solitary and utter responsibility of the recipient reader. Under no circumstances will any legal responsibility or blame be held against the publisher for any reparation, damages, or monetary loss due to the information herein, either directly or indirectly.

Respective authors own all copyrights not held by the publisher.

The information herein is offered for informational purposes solely, and is universal as so. The presentation of the information is without contract or any type of guarantee assurance.

The trademarks that are used are without any consent, and the publication of the trademark is without permission or backing by the trademark owner. All trademarks and brands within this book are for clarifying purposes only and are the owned by the owners themselves, not affiliated with this document.

TABLE OF CONTENTS

Chapter 1: Introduction to Greece
- Why Greece Should Be Your Next Destination
- Understanding Greece's Unique Geography
- A Brief Overview of Greece's Rich History
- The Greek Way of Life: Culture, Traditions, and Hospitality
- When to Visit: Seasons, Weather, and Festivals

Chapter 2: Athens – The Cradle of Western Civilization
- Exploring the Acropolis and Parthenon
- Must-Visit Museums: National Archaeological Museum and Beyond
- Strolling Through Plaka: Athens' Oldest Neighborhood
- Syntagma Square and the Changing of the Guard
- Modern Athens: Rooftop Bars and Local Markets
- Day Trips from Athens: Delphi, Cape Sounion, and More

Chapter 3: The Greek Islands – Paradise on Earth
- A Guide to the Cyclades: Santorini, Mykonos, and Naxos
- Crete: Beaches, Mountains, and Minoan History
- The Dodecanese Islands: Rhodes and Kos
- Ionian Islands: Corfu, Zakynthos, and Kefalonia

Chapter 4: Ancient Greece – Mythology and History Come to Life
- The Gods and Myths That Shaped a Civilization
- Olympia: Birthplace of the Olympic Games
- Delphi: The Oracle and the Center of the Ancient World
- Epidaurus: Theater, Healing, and Ancient Medicine
- Knossos and the Minoan Civilization
- Legendary Battles: Thermopylae, Marathon, and Salamis

Chapter 5: Greece's Stunning Natural Landscapes

- Meteora: Monasteries Suspended in the Sky
- Mount Olympus: Home of the Gods
- Vikos Gorge: Europe's Deepest Canyon
- The Blue Caves of Zakynthos
- Samaria Gorge: Crete's Hiking Haven
- Lake Plastira: A Hidden Gem in Central Greece

Chapter 6: Greek Cuisine – A Feast for the Senses

- An Introduction to Greek Food Culture
- Must-Try Dishes: Moussaka, Souvlaki, and Spanakopita
- Greek Desserts: Baklava, Loukoumades, and Beyond
- Wine and Spirits: Ouzo, Retsina, and Greek Wines
- The Art of the Greek Coffee and Meze Culture

Chapter 7: Modern Greece – Vibrant Cities and Contemporary Culture

- Thessaloniki: Greece's Cultural and Culinary Capital
- Patras: A Blend of History and Festivities
- Volos: Gateway to the Mythical Pelion
- Greece's Emerging Art and Music Scene
- Shopping in Greece: Local Crafts, Jewelry, and Souvenirs
- Greece's Nightlife: From Traditional Bouzoukia to Modern Clubs

Chapter 8: Final Thoughts and Reflections

- Reflecting on Greece's Magic
- Share Your Experience: Tips for Future Travelers

BONUS 1: Essential phrases for your daily travel needs in Greece

BONUS 2: Printable travel journal

BONUS 3: 10 tips "that can save the day" on your trip in Greece

CHAPTER 1: INTRODUCTION TO GREECE

Why Greece Should Be Your Next Destination

The allure of Greece transcends its iconic images of whitewashed houses with blue-domed roofs and endless stretches of turquoise seas. Greece is not merely a destination; it is an experience, a journey through time, culture, and natural wonders that offers something for every traveler. Its unique blend of ancient history, breathtaking landscapes, vibrant cities, and warm hospitality makes it a place where every visit feels like stepping into a living postcard. Beyond its aesthetic beauty, Greece captures the soul with its profound sense of history, its deeply rooted traditions, and the simple yet unparalleled joy of its way of life.

Few countries in the world can boast of the historical significance that Greece holds. This is the land where Western civilization was born, where democracy, philosophy, and the arts flourished. Walking through the ruins of the Acropolis in Athens, you are not just visiting an archaeological site but standing on ground where Socrates, Plato, and Aristotle once debated the very principles that shape modern society. The Parthenon, a symbol of architectural perfection, towers above the city, whispering tales of a civilization that valued beauty, innovation, and intellect. The stories of Greek mythology, woven into every corner of the land, add another layer of fascination. Whether it's the legend of Zeus ruling from Mount

Olympus or the tale of the Oracle of Delphi guiding ancient leaders, these myths breathe life into the stones and landscapes.

Beyond its historical treasures, Greece is a land of unparalleled natural beauty. The diversity of its geography is astounding. The Greek islands alone, scattered like jewels across the Aegean and Ionian seas, offer a staggering variety of experiences. Santorini's dramatic cliffs and caldera sunsets are a feast for the eyes, while Mykonos buzzes with energy, nightlife, and pristine beaches. The lush greenery of Corfu contrasts sharply with the rugged, untamed charm of Crete, where mountains meet azure waters. Lesser-known islands like Naxos and Milos offer quieter escapes, each with its unique landscapes and traditions. But it's not just the islands that captivate. The mainland is equally mesmerizing, with its towering mountains, serene lakes, and ancient forests. Meteora's monasteries perched atop rock pillars seem almost otherworldly, while the Vikos Gorge offers hiking trails through one of Europe's deepest canyons.

Greece is a haven for food lovers, and its cuisine alone is reason enough to make it your next destination. The flavors of Greek food are a reflection of the land itself: fresh, vibrant, and deeply satisfying. Meals in Greece are not just about eating; they are about community, sharing, and celebration. A simple Greek salad, bursting with the flavors of ripe tomatoes, crisp cucumbers, and briny feta cheese, tastes like summer on a plate. Slow-cooked lamb, marinated in herbs and olive oil, melts in your mouth, while fresh seafood, caught just hours before, is grilled to perfection and served with a squeeze of lemon. The meze culture, where small plates are shared among friends, turns every meal into a social event. And let's not forget the desserts—honey-drenched baklava, fluffy loukoumades, and creamy galaktoboureko are sweet enough to make you forget any diet. Pair it all with a glass of ouzo or a bottle of Assyrtiko wine, and you'll understand why food is such an integral part of Greek life.

The people of Greece are another reason to visit. Greeks are known for their philoxenia, a term that translates to "friend to a stranger" and embodies their spirit of hospitality. Whether you're in a bustling city or a remote mountain village, you'll be welcomed with open arms. Locals take pride in sharing their culture, traditions, and stories, often over a glass of raki or a cup of Greek coffee. This genuine warmth makes you feel less like a tourist and more like a guest in someone's home. It's not uncommon for strangers to become friends and for memories made in Greece to linger long after you've left.

The rhythm of life in Greece is another compelling draw. There's a certain magic in the way time seems to slow down here, allowing you to savor each moment. The Greeks have perfected the art of living well. Whether it's enjoying a leisurely meal by the sea, watching the sun dip below the horizon, or simply strolling through a village square, life in Greece encourages you to pause, breathe, and appreciate the beauty around you. This relaxed pace, combined with the country's natural beauty and rich culture, creates a sense of balance and well-being that is hard to find elsewhere.

For those seeking adventure, Greece offers a wealth of activities to satisfy any thrill-seeker. Dive into crystal-clear waters to explore underwater caves and shipwrecks, hike through ancient paths on Mount Olympus, or windsurf in the breezy bays of the Aegean. The varied terrain provides endless opportunities for outdoor exploration, from rock climbing in Kalymnos to horseback riding through the olive groves of the Peloponnese. Water sports enthusiasts can kayak around hidden coves, while history buffs can venture off the beaten path to discover forgotten ruins and Byzantine monasteries. Greece's natural and historical wonders are a playground for those eager to explore.

Seasonal festivals and celebrations add another layer of excitement to a visit to Greece. No matter the time of year, there's always something happening. In spring, the Orthodox Easter celebrations are a spectacle of traditions, processions, and feasts that bring communities together. Summer is alive with music and dance festivals, many set against the backdrop of ancient theaters and seaside stages. Autumn brings grape harvests and wine festivals, while winter, though quieter, offers a chance to experience Greek traditions in a more intimate setting. These events provide a glimpse into the heart of Greek culture and are a reminder of the importance of community and celebration.

Practicality is another reason to choose Greece as your next destination. The country is incredibly accessible, with an abundance of international flights, well-connected ferry systems, and a range of accommodations to suit every budget. Whether you're a backpacker looking for affordable hostels, a family seeking kid-friendly resorts, or a luxury traveler wanting private villas, Greece has options for everyone. The cost of living is relatively affordable compared to other

European destinations, making it possible to enjoy a high-quality experience without breaking the bank.

Safety is often a concern for travelers, but Greece is known for its low crime rates and welcoming atmosphere. It's a destination where you can wander the labyrinthine streets of an island village late at night or walk along Athens' lit-up monuments and feel entirely at ease. The Greek people's hospitality extends to ensuring visitors feel safe and comfortable, further enhancing the travel experience.

For anyone with an interest in art, literature, or philosophy, Greece is an endless source of inspiration. It's difficult not to feel moved while standing in the shadow of the Parthenon or gazing at the same sunsets that inspired Homer's epics. The country's cultural legacy is palpable, from the ancient amphitheaters that still host performances to the modern art galleries and literary festivals that continue to celebrate creativity. Greece is a bridge between the ancient and the modern, a place where the past informs the present in the most beautiful ways.

The intangible magic of Greece is hard to put into words. It's a feeling, a connection, an experience that stays with you. Whether it's the warmth of the sun on your skin, the sound of waves lapping against the shore, or the laughter shared over a meal with newfound friends, Greece has a way of leaving an indelible mark on your heart. It's a destination that invites you to lose yourself in its beauty, its history, and its way of life, only to find a deeper sense of connection, wonder, and joy.

Understanding Greece's Unique Geography

Greece's geography is an intricate tapestry woven together by dramatic landscapes, scattered islands, rugged mountains, and endless coastlines. Situated at the crossroads of Europe, Asia, and Africa, the country occupies the southernmost tip of the Balkan Peninsula and consists of a mainland, a peninsula known as the Peloponnese, and over 6,000 islands and islets spread across the Aegean and Ionian Seas. This unique geographical diversity is not only a defining characteristic of Greece but also a major factor in its historical, cultural, and economic development. Each region, whether on the mainland or among the islands, tells its own story through its topography, natural resources, and strategic location.

The mainland of Greece is a land of contrasts, dominated by mountains and intersected by fertile plains. Nearly 80% of the country is mountainous, making it one of the most mountainous nations in Europe. The Pindus mountain range, often referred to as the "spine of Greece," stretches across the mainland from the northwest to the southeast, forming dramatic peaks and deep valleys. These rugged landscapes provide not only breathtaking views but also a natural barrier that historically influenced the development of isolated city-states in ancient Greece. The highest peak, Mount Olympus, towers at 2,917 meters and holds a revered place in Greek mythology as the home of the gods. In the north, the Rhodope Mountains create a natural border with Bulgaria, their dense forests offering a haven for biodiversity and outdoor enthusiasts alike.

The plains of Thessaly and Macedonia break up the mountainous terrain, creating fertile regions that have been the agricultural heartland of Greece for centuries. These areas are dotted with vineyards, olive groves, and fields of wheat, showcasing the agricultural richness of the land. The rivers flowing through these plains, such as the Pinios and Axios, provide a lifeline for irrigation and support ecosystems teeming with life. The contrast between the soaring mountains and the productive lowlands exemplifies the diversity of Greece's mainland geography and its ability to sustain human habitation and growth despite its rugged nature.

One of the most defining features of Greece's geography is its extensive coastline, which stretches over 13,500 kilometers, making it the longest in the Mediterranean and among the longest in the world. The coastline is a mesmerizing blend of sandy beaches, rocky cliffs, secluded bays, and bustling harbors. The Aegean Sea to the east, the Ionian Sea to the west, and the Sea of Crete to the south surround the mainland and its islands, creating a maritime culture deeply ingrained in Greek identity. The sea has always been a source of sustenance, trade, and exploration for the Greeks, shaping their history and connecting them to distant lands.

The islands of Greece are perhaps its most famous geographical feature, with each group offering a distinct character and charm. The Cyclades, located in the central Aegean Sea, are known for their iconic whitewashed architecture, narrow cobblestone streets, and vibrant nightlife. Santorini, with its caldera views and volcanic beaches, is a postcard-perfect destination, while Mykonos attracts visitors with its cosmopolitan atmosphere and lively energy. Naxos and Paros, less crowded yet equally enchanting, offer a more authentic glimpse into Cycladic life with their rolling hills, ancient ruins, and traditional villages.

To the south lies Crete, the largest Greek island, which holds a unique place in the country's geography and culture. Its diverse landscapes range from sandy shores to rugged mountain ranges, such as the White Mountains and the Psiloritis range. Crete is also home to fertile plateaus like Lasithi, where windmills dot the landscape, and gorges such as Samaria, a hiker's paradise. The island's distinct identity is shaped by its size and position at the crossroads of three continents, making it a melting pot of influences and traditions.

The Ionian Islands, located off the western coast of mainland Greece in the Ionian Sea, contrast sharply with the Cyclades. Known for their lush greenery and Venetian architecture, islands like Corfu, Zakynthos, and Kefalonia exude a different kind of charm. Corfu's rolling hills and olive groves provide a serene escape, while Zakynthos' Navagio Beach, with its striking turquoise waters and shipwreck centerpiece, is one of the most photographed spots in Greece. Kefalonia, the largest of the Ionian Islands, offers diverse landscapes that include dramatic cliffs, underground lakes, and pristine beaches.

Further east, the Dodecanese Islands, located near the Turkish coast, offer a blend of Greek and Eastern influences. Rhodes, the largest and most well-known of this group, is famed for its medieval Old Town, a UNESCO World Heritage Site, and its stunning beaches. The island of Kos, with its ancient ruins and vibrant nightlife, and the smaller, quieter islands like Symi and Patmos, each have their unique appeal. The Sporades and North Aegean islands, less frequented by tourists, are hidden gems that boast unspoiled natural beauty, traditional villages, and a slower pace of life.

The Peloponnese peninsula, connected to the mainland by the Isthmus of Corinth, is a microcosm of Greece's geographical diversity. Its landscape includes rugged mountains, fertile valleys, and a jagged coastline dotted with picturesque towns and ancient sites. The Taygetus mountain range dominates the southern part of the peninsula, its peaks offering spectacular views and challenging hiking trails. The region is home to some of Greece's most significant historical landmarks, including the ancient theater of Epidaurus, the ruins of Mycenae, and the site of Olympia, the birthplace of the Olympic Games. The Mani Peninsula, with its wild beauty and traditional stone towers, feels like a world apart, offering a glimpse into a more remote and untouched side of Greece.

Greece's geography is not limited to its physical features but extends to its climate, which varies from region to region due to its diverse topography. The country enjoys a Mediterranean climate, characterized by hot, dry summers and mild, wet winters, particularly in coastal areas. However, the mountainous regions experience cooler temperatures and, in some cases, snow during the winter months, making Greece a year-round destination. The islands and coastal areas benefit from cooling sea breezes, while the mainland's interior can see more extreme temperatures. This climatic variety allows for a wide range of activities, from sunbathing on beaches to skiing in the mountains.

The unique geography of Greece has also played a crucial role in shaping its history and culture. The scattered islands and rugged terrain encouraged the development of independent city-states in ancient times, such as Athens, Sparta, and Corinth, each with its distinct character and governance. The seas that surround Greece facilitated trade, exploration, and cultural exchange, connecting the ancient Greeks with civilizations in Egypt, the Middle East, and beyond. The natural barriers of mountains and seas also provided protection from invasions, contributing to the preservation of Greek culture and identity through the centuries.

In modern times, Greece's geography continues to influence its economy and way of life. Tourism, driven largely by the country's stunning landscapes and coastline, is a major contributor to the economy. Agriculture remains vital, with olive oil, wine, and fresh produce being staples of Greek exports. The country's maritime tradition thrives, with Greece holding one of the largest merchant fleets in the world. The strategic location of Greece at the crossroads of continents makes it a critical player in regional politics and trade.

Understanding the geography of Greece is key to appreciating its allure and complexity. The interplay of mountains, seas, and islands creates a landscape that is as diverse as it is beautiful, offering endless opportunities for exploration and discovery. Each region, shaped by its unique geographical features, contributes to the rich tapestry of Greek culture and history. The geographical diversity of Greece is not just a backdrop for its stories; it is an integral part of the narrative, influencing everything from its ancient myths to its modern identity.

A Brief Overview of Greece's Rich History

Greece's history is a vast and complex narrative that spans thousands of years, shaping not only the nation itself but the very foundations of Western civilization. From the rise of the ancient Minoans to the intricate city-states of the Classical period, from the far-reaching conquests of Alexander the Great to the centuries of Ottoman rule, each era of Greece's history left an indelible mark on its culture, architecture, and identity. The story of Greece is one of resilience, reinvention, and cultural brilliance, where the past continues to echo in the present and influence the world at large.

The earliest chapter in Greece's history begins with the Minoan civilization, which flourished between 3000 and 1450 BCE on the island of Crete. As the first advanced civilization in Europe, the Minoans demonstrated remarkable achievements in architecture, art, and trade. The Palace of Knossos, with its intricate frescoes and advanced plumbing systems, stands as a testament to their ingenuity. The Minoans were a maritime people, establishing extensive trade networks that reached Egypt and Mesopotamia. Their art, characterized by vibrant depictions of nature and daily life, reveals a society that valued beauty and harmony. However, the mysterious decline of the Minoans, possibly due to a massive volcanic eruption on the nearby island of Thera (modern-day Santorini), marked the end of their dominance and paved the way for the rise of the Mycenaean civilization.

The Mycenaeans, centered on the Greek mainland, emerged as the dominant power around 1600 BCE. They are often associated with the legends of the Trojan War, immortalized in Homer's epic poems, the *Iliad* and the *Odyssey*. The Mycenaeans were warriors and builders, constructing massive fortresses such as the one at Mycenae, with its iconic Lion Gate. Their society was hierarchical, with powerful kings ruling over city-states. They adopted elements of Minoan culture, including their writing system, which evolved into Linear B—the earliest known form of written Greek. By 1100 BCE, however, the Mycenaean civilization collapsed, likely due to a combination of internal strife and external invasions, plunging Greece into a period of decline known as the Dark Ages.

The Dark Ages, spanning from around 1100 to 800 BCE, were a time of significant upheaval and transformation. While large-scale construction and writing disappeared, oral traditions flourished, preserving the myths and histories that would later define Greek culture. During this period, the foundations for the resurgence of Greek society were laid. Small agricultural communities began to grow, and by the 8th century BCE, the emergence of the polis, or city-state, heralded the beginning of the Archaic period.

The Archaic period (800–480 BCE) was a time of political, cultural, and artistic renewal. City-states such as Athens, Sparta, and Corinth began to take shape, each with its own distinct identity and governance. Colonization efforts expanded Greek influence across the Mediterranean and Black Seas, spreading their language and culture to regions as far as Italy and Asia Minor. This era also saw the development of the Greek alphabet, adapted from the Phoenicians, which made literacy more accessible and allowed for the recording of literature, laws, and other cultural achievements. The Archaic period is perhaps best remembered for the birth of monumental sculpture and architecture, including the kouros statues and the earliest temples dedicated to the gods.

The Classical period (480–323 BCE) is often regarded as the pinnacle of Greek civilization. It was during this time that Greece produced some of its most enduring contributions to art, philosophy, and governance. The period began with a remarkable show of unity among the Greek city-states during the Persian Wars, where they successfully repelled the invasions of the mighty Persian Empire. The victories at Marathon, Thermopylae, and Salamis demonstrated the strength and resilience of the Greeks and cemented their place in history.

Athens emerged as a cultural and intellectual hub during the Classical period, ushering in what is often referred to as the "Golden Age" under the leadership of Pericles. The city became a center of democracy, a revolutionary system of governance where citizens could participate directly in decision-making. Philosophers such as Socrates, Plato, and Aristotle laid the foundations of Western philosophy, exploring questions of ethics, logic, and the nature of existence. In the arts, playwrights like Sophocles, Euripides, and Aristophanes brought drama to new heights, while sculptors such as Phidias created masterpieces like the Parthenon.

The Classical period also witnessed fierce rivalries between city-states, most notably the Peloponnesian War between Athens and Sparta. This protracted conflict weakened the

Greek world and set the stage for the rise of Macedonia under Philip II and his son, Alexander the Great. Alexander's conquests in the late 4th century BCE marked the beginning of the Hellenistic period, a time when Greek culture spread across a vast empire that stretched from Egypt to India.

The Hellenistic period (323–31 BCE) was characterized by a blending of Greek and Eastern cultures, creating a cosmopolitan world where art, science, and philosophy flourished. Cities such as Alexandria in Egypt became centers of learning and innovation, housing institutions like the Great Library and attracting scholars from across the known world. Advances in mathematics, astronomy, and medicine were made by figures such as Euclid, Archimedes, and Hippocrates. Greek art and architecture took on new forms, emphasizing emotion and movement.

By 146 BCE, Greece had fallen under Roman control, becoming a province of the Roman Empire. However, rather than erasing Greek culture, the Romans admired and adopted many aspects of it, from their gods and architecture to their philosophy and literature. This period of Roman Greece, known as the Greco-Roman era, saw the continuation of Greek traditions alongside Roman innovations. The city of Athens remained a center of learning, attracting Roman elites who sought to emulate Greek ideals.

The Byzantine period (330–1453 CE) marked a new chapter in Greek history, as Greece became part of the Eastern Roman Empire. With the founding of Constantinople (modern-day Istanbul) as the empire's capital, the Byzantine period was defined by the spread of Christianity and the blending of

Roman, Greek, and Christian traditions. Byzantine art, particularly its mosaics and icons, reflected the deep spirituality of the time. Greek became the official language of the empire, preserving the cultural and intellectual heritage of ancient Greece.

Following the fall of Constantinople to the Ottoman Turks in 1453, Greece endured nearly four centuries of Ottoman rule. Despite the hardships, Greek culture and identity persisted, often finding expression through the Orthodox Church, which became a guardian of Greek traditions and language. The desire for independence grew over time, culminating in the Greek War of Independence in the early 19th century. The struggle for freedom, fueled by a renewed sense of national identity and support from European powers, led to the establishment of the modern Greek state in 1830.

Modern Greece has since undergone significant transformations, weathering wars, political upheavals, and economic challenges. Yet, it has remained a beacon of cultural heritage and resilience. The country's history is not just a record of its past but a living presence that continues to shape its people and inspire the world. Each era, from the Minoans to the Byzantines, from the Classical philosophers to the modern revolutionaries, has contributed to the rich tapestry of Greek history, making it a story of enduring significance and universal appeal.

The Greek Way of Life: Culture, Traditions, and Hospitality

The Greek way of life is a harmonious blend of ancient traditions and modern influences, creating a culture that is as vibrant as it is timeless. It is a mosaic of customs, values, and beliefs that have been shaped over millennia, rooted in history yet constantly evolving. Central to this way of life are the principles of community, hospitality, and an unwavering connection to the past. Greece is not simply a place; it is a way of being, where life is celebrated in all its forms, and where the smallest moments are infused with meaning and joy.

At the heart of Greek culture lies the concept of *philoxenia*, a word that translates to "friend of the stranger." This idea of hospitality is not just a practice but a deeply ingrained philosophy that transcends time. Whether you find yourself in a bustling city or a remote mountain village, you are likely to be welcomed with open arms, often accompanied by an offer of food or drink. This generosity is not reserved for guests staying in homes; it extends to strangers passing through, travelers in need, and even casual acquaintances. It is not uncommon for Greeks to invite visitors into their homes for a meal, treating them like family regardless of how brief the acquaintance may be. This spirit of hospitality has its roots in ancient Greek mythology, where the gods often tested mortals by appearing as strangers in need, rewarding those who showed kindness and punishing those who did not.

Family plays an essential role in the Greek way of life, serving as the foundation of social structure and personal identity. Strong familial bonds are evident in every aspect of life, from the multigenerational households where grandparents often live with their children and grandchildren, to the frequent family gatherings that mark celebrations and milestones. These gatherings are lively affairs, filled with laughter, stories, and, of course, food. Greek families take pride in their heritage, passing down traditions, recipes, and stories from one generation to the next. The sense of belonging and support provided by family extends beyond blood relations, as close friends are often considered part of the family circle.

Religion is another cornerstone of Greek culture, with the Greek Orthodox Church playing a significant role in the lives of many. While modern Greece is a secular state, religious traditions and rituals remain deeply woven into the fabric of daily life. Churches and chapels, often adorned with stunning frescoes and icons, are found in every corner of the country, from the smallest islands to the largest cities. Major religious holidays, such as Easter, are celebrated with an intensity and reverence that bring communities together. The Easter celebration, in particular, is a profound experience, beginning with a solemn Holy Week and culminating in a joyous feast marked by roasted lamb, red-dyed eggs, and traditional dances. Religious festivals dedicated to saints are also common, often accompanied by music, food, and dancing that can last well into the night.

Food is not merely sustenance in Greece; it is an expression of culture, a way to connect with others, and a form of art. Meals are a time to gather, share stories, and enjoy the bounty of the land and sea. Greek cuisine is characterized by its simplicity, relying on fresh, high-quality ingredients such as olive oil, tomatoes, lemons, and herbs. Traditional dishes like moussaka, souvlaki, and spanakopita are staples, while regional specialties showcase the diversity of the country's culinary heritage. Dining in Greece is a leisurely affair, often stretching for hours as plates of meze are shared and wine or ouzo flows freely. In villages, it is common to see locals gathering at the *kafeneio*, or coffee house, to sip Greek coffee and exchange news, a practice that embodies the importance of community and connection in everyday life.

Music and dance are integral to Greek culture, serving as both a form of expression and a means of bringing people together. Traditional Greek music, with its distinct melodies and rhythms, often features instruments like the bouzouki, lyra, and clarinet. These sounds are not confined to formal performances; they are a part of daily life, whether at a wedding, a festival, or a simple gathering of friends. Greek dances, such as the *sirtaki* and *kalamatianos*, are communal activities that invite participation regardless of age or skill level. The circular formation of many dances symbolizes unity and equality, reflecting the collective spirit that is so central to Greek life.

Seasonal festivals and celebrations are a vibrant aspect of Greek culture, offering a glimpse into the customs and traditions that define each region. These events often revolve around religious holidays, agricultural cycles, or historical commemorations. One such example is the *panigyri*, a festive gathering typically held in honor of a patron saint. These celebrations feature live music, dancing, and feasting, transforming village squares into lively hubs of activity. Carnival season, known as *Apokries*, is another highlight, marked by colorful parades, costumes, and masquerade balls that bring communities together in a spirit of playfulness and creativity.

The Greek connection to nature is evident in the way people interact with the land and sea. Agriculture remains a significant part of life in rural areas, where olive groves, vineyards, and citrus orchards dominate the landscape. The sea, too, plays a vital role, providing not only sustenance but also a sense of identity for coastal communities. Fishermen can often be seen mending their nets by the harbor, while families gather on the beach to enjoy the simple pleasures of sun, sand, and water. This closeness to nature is reflected in Greek proverbs, poetry, and even the rhythm of daily life, which often follows the cycles of the seasons.

The Greek concept of *kefi*—a word that loosely translates to joy, spirit, or passion—captures the essence of Greek culture. It is the unspoken energy that drives a spontaneous dance, the laughter that echoes through a taverna late at night, or the deep sense of contentment found in a shared moment with loved ones. *Kefi* cannot be forced or manufactured; it arises naturally, often in the most unexpected moments. It is a reminder to live fully, to embrace life's beauty and challenges with equal enthusiasm, and to find joy in the present.

Despite the pressures of modernization and globalization, Greece has managed to preserve its traditions while adapting to the demands of the modern world. Urban centers like Athens and Thessaloniki are hubs of contemporary art, music, and gastronomy, yet they remain deeply connected to their cultural roots. This blending of old and new is evident in the way ancient ruins coexist with modern architecture, or how traditional recipes are reimagined in innovative ways by young chefs. The Greek spirit of resilience, creativity, and adaptability ensures that its culture remains vibrant and relevant.

The simplicity and depth of Greek life offer lessons that resonate far beyond its borders. It is a culture that values connection over convenience, experience over material possessions, and tradition over fleeting trends. Whether through the warmth of a stranger's welcome, the rhythm of a traditional dance, or the taste of a lovingly prepared meal, the Greek way of life invites us to slow down, savor the moment, and find joy in the everyday. It is a reminder that life's greatest treasures are often the simplest ones, shared with others in the spirit of *philoxenia* and *kefi*. In Greece, life is not just lived—it is celebrated.

When to Visit: Seasons, Weather, and Festivals

Greece is a country that offers something magical in every season, and knowing when to visit can greatly enhance your experience depending on your interests, preferences, and what you hope to discover. The country's diverse geography creates a variety of microclimates, and its cultural calendar is packed with festivals and events that bring communities to life. To determine the ideal time to visit, it's important to consider what you want from your journey—whether it's sun-drenched beaches, ancient ruins without the crowds, or an authentic taste of Greek traditions during local festivals.

The summer months, from June to August, are the peak of the tourist season in Greece, and for good reason. This is when the country's islands and coastal regions truly shine. The Aegean and Ionian Seas are warm and inviting, perfect for swimming, snorkeling, and other water activities. The Cyclades islands, including Santorini and Mykonos, are bustling with life, with restaurants, bars, and shops in full swing. The long daylight hours allow visitors to maximize their time exploring or relaxing, and the consistent sunshine creates the idyllic conditions that many associate with a Greek summer. However, the popularity of this season means that major tourist destinations can become crowded, and prices for accommodations and flights often reach their highest points. Travelers seeking solitude or a quieter experience may find it challenging to escape the throngs of visitors on the more well-known islands. That said, even during the height of summer, lesser-known destinations like Karpathos, Amorgos, or the Mani Peninsula offer a more tranquil escape, with equally stunning landscapes and warm hospitality.

The heat of the Greek summer is something to consider, particularly for those planning to explore historical sites or engage in outdoor activities. Temperatures in July and August can soar past 35°C (95°F), especially in mainland regions like Athens or the Peloponnese. Walking through the Acropolis under the blazing sun can become physically demanding, so it's essential to plan visits to archaeological sites early in the morning or late in the afternoon. Coastal regions and the islands benefit from cooling sea breezes, but inland areas may feel stifling during midday. Lightweight clothing, plenty of water, and sunscreen are necessities if you visit during this period.

Spring, spanning from mid-March to May, is arguably one of the best times to visit Greece. As the country awakens from its winter slumber, the landscape bursts into life with wildflowers carpeting the hills and olive groves. The weather during this season is mild and pleasant, with average temperatures ranging from 15°C to 25°C (59°F to 77°F), making it ideal for hiking, sightseeing, and outdoor activities. Popular historical sites such as Delphi, Epidaurus, and Olympia are far less crowded than they are in summer, allowing you to enjoy them at a leisurely pace. The islands are beginning to open up for the season, but without the large crowds of summer, you'll have more space to explore their beaches, villages, and trails.

Spring is also the season of Easter, which is the most important religious celebration in Greece. The week leading up to Orthodox Easter, known as Holy Week, is filled with solemn rituals, processions, and traditions that culminate in a joyous celebration on Easter Sunday. Villages and towns across the country come alive with festivities, including outdoor feasts featuring roasted lamb, music, and dancing. Experiencing Easter in Greece offers a unique insight into the country's deep-rooted traditions and sense of community. Smaller islands and rural areas are particularly enchanting during this time, as locals welcome visitors to join in their celebrations.

Autumn, from September to November, rivals spring as one of the most favorable times to visit Greece. The crowds of summer have thinned, the intense heat has subsided, and the sea remains warm enough for swimming well into October. September is particularly delightful, as it combines the pleasant weather of late summer with a more relaxed atmosphere. Grapes, figs, and other seasonal fruits are harvested during this period, adding a touch of authenticity to the culinary experiences you'll encounter. The grape harvest is often accompanied by wine festivals in regions like Nemea and Crete, where visitors can participate in traditional grape-stomping ceremonies and sample local wines.

Autumn also offers excellent conditions for hiking and exploring Greece's natural landscapes. The Samaria Gorge in Crete, the Vikos Gorge in Epirus, and the trails of Mount Olympus are less crowded than in summer, allowing you to fully immerse yourself in the beauty of the surroundings. The cooler temperatures make it easier to undertake longer treks, and the changing colors of the foliage add a unique charm to the scenery. Cultural events, such as the Athens International Film Festival in September and the Dimitria Festival in Thessaloniki, offer a chance to experience Greece's thriving contemporary arts scene alongside its ancient heritage.

Winter, from December to February, is often overlooked by travelers but holds its own special appeal. While the islands enter a quieter phase and many tourist-oriented businesses close for the season, mainland Greece reveals a different side of its character. Athens remains lively year-round, with its museums, galleries, and archaeological sites offering a wealth of indoor activities. The city's café culture thrives during the colder months, providing cozy spots to relax and savor Greek coffee or a warm cup of *rakomelo*, a traditional drink made from honey and raki.

For those who enjoy winter sports, Greece has several ski resorts, such as Parnassos near Delphi and Kalavrita in the Peloponnese. These destinations are popular with locals and provide an opportunity to experience Greece's mountainous regions in a completely different light. Winter is also a time for cultural and religious festivals, including Christmas and Epiphany, both celebrated with unique Greek traditions. On Epiphany, which falls on January 6th, coastal towns hold the "Blessing of the Waters," where a cross is thrown into the sea and brave swimmers dive in to retrieve it, symbolizing purification and renewal.

The island of Crete deserves special mention when discussing the ideal time to visit Greece. Its southern location and varied topography create a microclimate that allows for pleasant weather nearly year-round. Even in winter, Crete's coastal areas remain mild, while its mountainous regions offer opportunities for snow-covered exploration. Spring and autumn are particularly delightful on Crete, with blooming wildflowers in the former and the olive harvest in the latter providing a glimpse into the island's agricultural traditions.

Festivals and events occur throughout the year in Greece, adding an extra layer of richness to your visit. The Athens and Epidaurus Festival, held from June to August, brings world-class performances of theater, music, and dance to historic venues such as the Odeon of Herodes Atticus and the ancient theater of Epidaurus. Carnival season, leading up to Lent in February or March, features parades, costumes, and lively celebrations, particularly in cities like Patras, which hosts one of Europe's largest carnival events. Smaller, regional festivals often dedicated to saints or agricultural traditions, provide a more intimate and authentic experience. These events are an opportunity to connect with locals, enjoy traditional music and dancing, and sample regional delicacies.

Choosing the best time to visit Greece ultimately depends on your preferences and what you hope to experience. Each season offers its own unique charms, from the sun-soaked vibrancy of summer to the tranquil beauty of winter. By aligning your trip with the season that best suits your interests, you can discover the many facets of Greece's timeless allure, whether it's through its natural landscapes, cultural traditions, or simply the warmth of its people. Every time of year reveals a different layer of this extraordinary country, offering endless reasons to return and explore further.

CHAPTER 2: ATHENS – THE CRADLE OF WESTERN CIVILIZATION

Exploring the Acropolis and Parthenon

Rising majestically above the heart of Athens, the Acropolis is a symbol of ancient Greece, a testament to its cultural and architectural achievements, and one of the most iconic landmarks in the world. Visiting the Acropolis and its crowning jewel, the Parthenon, is not merely an excursion but an immersion into the history, mythology, and artistry of a civilization that laid the foundations for Western culture. The experience of standing on this sacred rock, surrounded by monuments that have endured for millennia, is awe-inspiring, offering a glimpse into the brilliance of ancient Athens and its enduring legacy.

The Acropolis, meaning "high city," served as the epicenter of Athenian life in ancient times, both physically and spiritually. Its elevated position made it an ideal location for fortifications during the Mycenaean period, but it was during the 5th century BCE, under the leadership of Pericles, that it took on the form we recognize today. The Acropolis became a monumental complex dedicated to Athena, the city's patron goddess, and a showcase of Athenian power, wealth, and artistic excellence. The construction of the Parthenon, the Propylaea, the Erechtheion, and the Temple of Athena Nike transformed the site into a masterpiece of classical architecture, each structure contributing to a harmonious whole.

As you ascend the hill toward the Acropolis, the anticipation builds with each step. The journey begins at the base, where the ancient city's remains blend seamlessly with the modern urban landscape of Athens. The climb is not merely a path to the past but a physical connection to the countless individuals who have walked this route over the centuries. The effort of the ascent is rewarded with sweeping views of the city below, stretching to the Aegean Sea in the distance, a reminder of Athens' strategic location and its historical significance as a maritime power.

At the entrance to the Acropolis stands the Propylaea, the grand gateway that once welcomed visitors to this sacred precinct. Designed by the architect Mnesicles, this monumental structure is a masterpiece of symmetry and proportion, blending Doric and Ionic architectural elements. Though partially ruined, the Propylaea still conveys a sense of grandeur, its marble columns gleaming in the sunlight. Passing through its central hall feels like stepping into another realm, a transition from the bustling modern city to the sanctity of ancient Athens.

To the right of the Propylaea lies the Temple of Athena Nike, a small but exquisitely crafted structure dedicated to Athena as the goddess of victory. Perched on a bastion overlooking the Athenian plain, this Ionic temple once housed a statue of Athena holding a pomegranate and a helmet, symbols of peace and war. The friezes that adorned the temple depicted scenes of battles, celebrating Athens' military triumphs. Though the original sculptures are now housed in the Acropolis Museum, the temple itself remains a delicate and elegant reminder of the artistry of ancient Greek architects and sculptors.

The Parthenon, the centerpiece of the Acropolis, is a marvel of engineering and design that continues to captivate scholars and visitors alike. Built between 447 and 432 BCE under the direction of the architects Iktinos and Kallikrates and the sculptor Phidias, the Parthenon was dedicated to Athena Parthenos, the virgin goddess. Its Doric columns, adorned with subtle curvature to correct optical illusions, create an illusion of perfect straightness, a testament to the ingenuity of its creators. The temple originally housed a colossal statue of Athena crafted by Phidias, made of gold and ivory, a symbol of Athenian pride and devotion.

Walking around the Parthenon, you can appreciate the intricate details of its architecture and the monumental scale of its construction. The metopes and friezes that once adorned its exterior depicted scenes from Greek mythology, including the battle between the gods and the giants, the Trojan War, and the Panathenaic procession, a festival held in honor of Athena. Though many of these sculptures were removed during the Ottoman period and are now displayed in museums such as the British Museum and the Acropolis Museum, the remaining fragments still evoke the grandeur of the original design. The play of light and shadow on the marble, the contrast between the solid columns and the open spaces they frame, and the commanding view of Athens below all contribute to the Parthenon's enduring allure.

Adjacent to the Parthenon stands the Erechtheion, a complex and enigmatic structure that combines religious, mythological, and architectural significance. This Ionic temple is best known for its Caryatids, six sculpted female figures that serve as columns supporting the southern porch. Each Caryatid is uniquely detailed, their draped garments and graceful stances embodying the elegance of ancient Greek sculpture. The Erechtheion was dedicated to both Athena and Poseidon, reflecting the mythological contest between the two gods for the patronage of Athens. According to legend, Athena's gift of the olive tree, symbolizing peace and prosperity, won the favor of the Athenians, a story that resonates in the olive groves that still dot the landscape today.

Exploring the Acropolis is not limited to its architectural wonders; it is also an opportunity to delve into the mythology and history that permeate the site. The sacred rock has been a witness to countless events, from the golden age of Athens to its conquest by the Romans, its transformation under Byzantine and Ottoman rule, and its rediscovery during the modern era. Each layer of history adds depth to the experience, inviting visitors to reflect on the enduring significance of this place.

A visit to the Acropolis is incomplete without a stop at the Acropolis Museum, located at the foot of the hill. This state-of-the-art facility houses a treasure trove of artifacts uncovered during excavations, providing invaluable context for the monuments above. The museum's design, with its glass floors revealing ancient ruins and its top-floor gallery aligned with the Parthenon, creates a seamless connection between the past and the present. Highlights include the original Caryatids, meticulously restored and displayed in a way that allows visitors to appreciate their craftsmanship up close, and the Parthenon sculptures, arranged to evoke their original placement on the temple.

Timing your visit to the Acropolis can greatly enhance your experience. Early morning or late afternoon offers cooler temperatures and softer light, ideal for photography and avoiding the peak crowds. Comfortable footwear is essential for navigating the uneven terrain, and bringing water and sunscreen is advisable, especially during the warmer months. Guided tours or audio guides can provide valuable insights into the history and significance of the site, enriching your understanding and appreciation of its wonders.

The Acropolis and the Parthenon are more than just monuments; they are symbols of human achievement, resilience, and creativity. Standing amidst these ancient ruins, you can feel the weight of history and the spirit of a civilization that continues to inspire. The artistry, innovation, and ideals that shaped these structures remain relevant today, reminding us of the potential for greatness and the enduring power of cultural heritage. Exploring the Acropolis is not merely a journey through time; it is an encounter with the essence of what it means to be human.

Must-Visit Museums: National Archaeological Museum and Beyond

Athens is a city where history breathes through every corner, and its museums are a gateway to understanding the richness of its past and the cultural evolution that shaped Western civilization. From ancient relics to Byzantine treasures, the museums of Athens preserve and showcase the essence of Greece's identity. Among them, the National Archaeological Museum stands as a colossal repository of ancient artifacts, a place where the grandeur of antiquity is laid bare. Yet, beyond its walls, Athens offers a host of other exceptional museums that cater to diverse interests, each offering a unique lens through which to explore the city's heritage and artistry.

The National Archaeological Museum is not just the largest museum in Greece; it is one of the most important archaeological museums in the world. Located in the heart of Athens, its neoclassical façade gives way to a sprawling interior that houses over 11,000 exhibits spanning millennia. Walking through its halls is akin to embarking on a journey through time, starting from the prehistoric era and culminating in the late antiquity. The museum is organized thematically and chronologically, allowing visitors to navigate through the cultural milestones of ancient Greece with clarity and ease.

One of the most captivating sections of the National Archaeological Museum is the prehistoric collection, which includes artifacts from the Cycladic, Minoan, and Mycenaean civilizations. The Cycladic figurines, with their minimalist forms and enigmatic expressions, are among the most iconic pieces. Crafted from marble and dating back to as early as 3000 BCE, these figurines are thought to have served religious or funerary purposes, though their precise significance remains a mystery. The Mycenaean treasures, on the other hand, offer a glimpse into the opulence of this ancient warrior culture. The gold funerary mask known as the "Mask of Agamemnon," attributed to the legendary king of Homeric fame, stands out as a highlight, its delicate craftsmanship and hauntingly human features captivating all who see it.

The sculpture collection is another must-see, featuring masterpieces from the Archaic, Classical, and Hellenistic periods. The evolution of Greek art is vividly illustrated here, from the rigid forms of early kouroi statues to the dynamic poses of later works. The Artemision Bronze, a larger-than-life statue of either Zeus or Poseidon, is a marvel of artistic and technical skill. Discovered in a shipwreck off the coast of Euboea, the statue's outstretched arm and commanding stance convey a sense of power and motion that feels almost alive. Similarly, the statue of Aphrodite and Pan, depicting a playful and provocative scene, showcases the humor and humanity that permeated Hellenistic art.

The museum's vast collection of pottery and vases provides another window into ancient Greek life. These vessels, adorned with intricate black-figure and red-figure designs, depict scenes from mythology, daily activities, and social rituals. They serve not only as artistic achievements but also as historical documents, offering insights into the values, beliefs, and practices of the time. The detail and precision of the imagery, from depictions of Olympian gods to athletes in mid-contest, highlight the sophistication of ancient Greek artisans.

Beyond the National Archaeological Museum, Athens is home to a wealth of other museums that cater to specific interests and periods of Greek history. The Acropolis Museum, located at the foot of the Acropolis hill, is a modern architectural masterpiece that complements the ancient wonders it houses. Its glass floors reveal the ruins of an ancient Athenian neighborhood, connecting visitors to the site's layered history from the moment they step inside. The museum's crowning feature is its top-floor gallery, designed to replicate the dimensions and orientation of the Parthenon. Here, the Parthenon sculptures are displayed in a layout that evokes their original placement, accompanied by multimedia presentations that provide context and interpretation. The contrast between the sleek, contemporary design of the museum and the timeless beauty of the artifacts creates a striking visual and emotional experience.

For those interested in Byzantine and Christian art, the Byzantine and Christian Museum offers a comprehensive collection that spans the early Christian period to the post-Byzantine era. Housed in a historic villa, the museum's exhibits include religious icons, mosaics, manuscripts, and textiles that reflect the spiritual and artistic achievements of Byzantine culture. The serene ambiance of the museum, coupled with its beautifully curated displays, provides a deeper understanding of the continuity and transformation of Greek art and religion through the centuries.

The Museum of Cycladic Art is another gem, focusing on the art and culture of the Cycladic islands during the Bronze Age. Its compact yet meticulously curated collection highlights the distinctive aesthetic of Cycladic figurines, pottery, and tools. The museum also hosts temporary exhibitions that explore connections between Cycladic art and other ancient cultures, as well as its influence on modern artists such as Picasso and Brancusi. The elegant design of the museum itself, with its clean lines and harmonious layout, mirrors the simplicity and sophistication of the artifacts it houses.

For a more eclectic experience, the Benaki Museum offers a panoramic view of Greek history and culture from antiquity to the modern era. Its main building, housed in a neoclassical mansion, features an extensive collection that includes ancient artifacts, Byzantine icons, Ottoman textiles, and 19th-century Greek folk art. The museum's diverse exhibits reflect the complex and multifaceted identity of Greece, showcasing how its cultural heritage has been shaped by both internal continuity and external influences. The Benaki Museum also operates several satellite locations, each focusing on specific themes, such as Islamic art, contemporary Greek artists, or the history of toys.

The National Historical Museum, located in the Old Parliament House, is a treasure trove of artifacts related to modern Greek history. Its exhibits cover pivotal events such as the Greek War of Independence, the Balkan Wars, and World War II, offering a deeper understanding of the struggles and triumphs that have shaped Greece in recent centuries. The museum's collection includes weapons, uniforms, documents, and personal belongings of key figures, bringing to life the stories of those who fought for Greece's independence and sovereignty.

For a more contemporary perspective, the National Museum of Contemporary Art (EMST) is a dynamic space dedicated to modern and contemporary art. Situated in a repurposed industrial building, the museum showcases works by Greek and international artists, exploring themes such as identity, migration, and social change. The EMST's innovative exhibitions and installations provide a thought-provoking counterpoint to the city's ancient treasures, demonstrating the ongoing vitality of Greek creativity.

Athens' wealth of museums ensures that there is something to captivate every visitor, whether you are drawn to the mysteries of antiquity, the spirituality of Byzantine art, or the bold expressions of contemporary culture. Each museum offers not only a collection of artifacts but also a narrative that enriches your understanding of Greece's history, art, and identity. By exploring these cultural institutions, you gain a deeper appreciation for the complexity and continuity of Greek civilization, as well as its enduring influence on the world. The museums of Athens are not merely repositories of the past; they are living bridges to the present, inviting you to discover, reflect, and be inspired.

Strolling Through Plaka: Athens' Oldest Neighborhood

Nestled in the shadow of the Acropolis, Plaka is Athens' oldest and most charming neighborhood, a labyrinth of narrow, winding streets that transport visitors back in time. Known as the "Neighborhood of the Gods," its cobblestone paths, neoclassical mansions, vibrant bougainvillea, and ancient ruins make it a must-visit destination for anyone exploring the city. Strolling through Plaka is more than a sightseeing experience; it's a sensory journey where history, culture, and daily life blend seamlessly. The neighborhood embodies the spirit of Athens, offering a glimpse into its past while remaining a lively hub of activity in the present.

The origins of Plaka date back to antiquity, and evidence of its ancient roots can be found throughout the area. It was once part of the ancient city of Athens, and its streets are layered with history, from the classical period to Byzantine, Ottoman, and modern times. Walking through Plaka, you may come across fragments of ancient walls, Roman ruins, and Byzantine churches, each bearing witness to the neighborhood's long and varied history. The name "Plaka" is thought to derive from the ancient Greek word *plakos*, meaning "flat stone," possibly referring to the stone-paved streets that have endured for centuries.

Entering Plaka feels like stepping into another world, one where time flows differently. The streets are a delightful maze, with each turn revealing something new—a hidden courtyard, a quaint café, or a shop selling handmade crafts. The absence of cars in much of the neighborhood enhances the sense of tranquility, allowing you to fully appreciate the sights and sounds around you. Plaka's charm lies in its contrasts: the blend of old and new, the peaceful atmosphere of its quieter corners juxtaposed with the lively energy of its main thoroughfares.

One of the most striking features of Plaka is its architecture. The neighborhood is home to an array of neoclassical buildings, many of which date back to the 19th century when Athens became the capital of the modern Greek state. These elegant homes, with their pastel façades, wrought-iron balconies, and terracotta roofs, reflect the influence of European styles while retaining a distinctly Greek character. Many of these buildings have been lovingly restored and now house museums, art galleries, and boutique hotels, adding to the neighborhood's eclectic charm.

As you wander through Plaka, you'll inevitably stumble upon Anafiotika, a tiny enclave perched on the northeastern slopes of the Acropolis. This hidden gem feels like a slice of the Cyclades transported to the heart of Athens. Built in the mid-19th century by workers from the island of Anafi who came to Athens to help construct King Otto's palace, Anafiotika is characterized by its whitewashed houses, narrow alleys, and vibrant blue shutters. The area exudes a sense of serenity, and its elevated position offers stunning views of the city below. Anafiotika is a reminder of the deep connections between Athens and the islands, a testament to the enduring influence of Cycladic culture.

Plaka is also a treasure trove for history enthusiasts, with several important archaeological sites scattered throughout the neighborhood. One of the most prominent is the Roman Agora, an open-air marketplace built during the Roman period. The site includes the impressive Gate of Athena Archegetis, a monumental entrance that once welcomed traders and visitors. Nearby, the Tower of the Winds, an octagonal structure adorned with reliefs depicting the eight winds, served as an ancient timekeeping device and weather station. These remnants of the past serve as a tangible link to the lives and activities of those who inhabited Athens centuries ago.

The neighborhood's Byzantine heritage is equally evident in its many churches, some of which date back to the 10th and 11th centuries. The Church of Saint Nicholas Rangavas, with its distinctive bell tower and serene courtyard, is a fine example of Byzantine architecture. Inside, you'll find beautiful frescoes and icons that reflect the spiritual and artistic traditions of the era. The nearby Church of the Metamorphosis, or the Transfiguration, is another gem, its simple exterior belying the rich history within. These places of worship, often tucked away in quiet corners, offer a moment of reflection amid the bustling streets.

Plaka is also a paradise for food lovers, with its abundance of traditional tavernas, modern eateries, and street food vendors. Dining in Plaka is an opportunity to savor the flavors of Greece, from classic dishes like moussaka and souvlaki to regional specialties prepared with fresh, local ingredients. Many tavernas feature outdoor seating under the shade of grapevines or bougainvillea, creating a picturesque setting for a leisurely meal. Some of the most memorable dining experiences in Plaka are found in its smaller, family-run establishments, where recipes are passed down through generations and hospitality is a way of life.

Beyond its culinary delights, Plaka offers a vibrant shopping scene, with a mix of traditional and contemporary offerings. The neighborhood is famous for its handmade goods, including jewelry, ceramics, and textiles. Many of these items are crafted by local artisans, making them unique souvenirs that carry a piece of Athens' creative spirit. Plaka's shops also include antique stores and galleries showcasing the work of modern Greek artists, reflecting the neighborhood's role as a hub of artistic expression.

Evenings in Plaka are magical, as the neighborhood takes on a different character. The warm glow of streetlights and the soft hum of conversation create an inviting atmosphere, perfect for an after-dinner stroll or a drink at one of the area's bars. Live music is a common feature in many establishments, ranging from traditional Greek folk songs to contemporary performances. This blend of old and new, of tradition and innovation, is what makes Plaka a living, breathing part of Athens' cultural fabric.

For those seeking a deeper understanding of the neighborhood's history and culture, guided tours and walking tours are widely available. These experiences often include visits to lesser-known sites, storytelling that brings the area's history to life, and insights into the daily lives of its residents. Whether you choose to explore Plaka on your own or with a guide, the neighborhood's charm lies in its ability to surprise and delight with every step.

Plaka is more than just a neighborhood; it is the soul of Athens, a place where the city's past and present intersect. Its streets tell stories of ancient philosophers, Byzantine priests, Ottoman merchants, and modern-day Athenians, all of whom have left their mark on this remarkable area. As you stroll through Plaka, you become part of its ongoing story, adding your footsteps to the countless others who have walked these streets before you. It is a place that invites exploration, reflection, and connection, a reminder of the timeless beauty and enduring spirit of Athens.

Syntagma Square and the Changing of the Guard

Syntagma Square lies at the very heart of Athens, a vibrant and bustling hub that serves as both a historical landmark and a modern meeting point. Surrounded by grand architecture, luxury hotels, and popular cafés, the square is not only a central point in the city's geography but also in its cultural and political life. It is a place where history and tradition meet the rhythms of contemporary urban life. For visitors, Syntagma Square offers a unique opportunity to dive into Athens' multifaceted identity, with one of its most iconic attractions being the Changing of the Guard ceremony at the Tomb of the Unknown Soldier.

The square takes its name from the Greek word "Syntagma," meaning "Constitution," a reference to the pivotal 1843 uprising that forced King Otto of Greece to grant the country its first constitution. This historical moment set the tone for the square's role as a symbol of democracy and public expression. Today, Syntagma Square remains a focal point for political gatherings, cultural events, and daily life, embodying the spirit of Athens as a city that bridges its ancient past with its modern aspirations.

Dominating the eastern side of the square is the Hellenic Parliament building, an imposing neoclassical structure originally built as a royal palace in the 19th century. Its pale yellow façade and symmetrical design reflect the architectural trends of the era, while its current function as the seat of Greece's parliament underscores its importance in the country's democratic system. The wide plaza in front of the Parliament building serves as the stage for the Changing of the Guard, a ceremony that draws both tourists and locals to witness this display of tradition and discipline.

The Tomb of the Unknown Soldier, located directly in front of the Parliament, is a monument dedicated to the countless

Greek soldiers who have given their lives in battle without recognition. Carved into the marble of the monument is a bas-relief of a dying hoplite, a soldier of ancient Greece, connecting the sacrifices of modern soldiers to the storied military traditions of the classical era. Flanking the monument are inscriptions of key battles from Greek history, serving as a reminder of the country's enduring struggle for freedom and sovereignty. This site is more than a memorial; it is a symbol of national pride and collective memory.

The Changing of the Guard is performed by the Evzones, an elite ceremonial unit of the Hellenic Army. Known for their distinctive uniforms, the Evzones are immediately recognizable by their white foustanella (a pleated skirt with 400 folds symbolizing the 400 years of Ottoman occupation), their red tasseled caps, and their tsarouhia, traditional leather clogs with pom-poms. Every detail of their attire reflects Greece's cultural heritage, with elements dating back to the War of Independence in the early 19th century. The uniform is not merely ceremonial; it is a carefully crafted tribute to the nation's history and identity.

The ceremony takes place every hour, on the hour, but it is the Sunday morning version, held at 11 a.m., that offers the most elaborate spectacle. During this weekly highlight, the Evzones are accompanied by a full military band, and the guards perform a highly choreographed routine that combines precision, discipline, and ritual. The careful synchronization of their movements, from the high kicks to the deliberate placement of their rifles, creates a sense of solemnity and reverence. Each step is slow and deliberate, emphasizing the gravity of their role as guardians of the nation's memory.

Observing the Changing of the Guard allows a deeper appreciation for the traditions and values that define Greece. The ceremony is not merely a tourist attraction; it is a living expression of respect for those who have served and sacrificed for the country. Watching the guards, who remain stoic and unmoving even in the face of curious onlookers and camera flashes, is a humbling experience. Their unwavering focus and commitment to their duty serve as a powerful metaphor for the resilience of the Greek spirit.

Syntagma Square itself is a microcosm of Athens, offering a dynamic blend of history, culture, and daily life. The square is often filled with the energy of people coming and going, whether they are commuters catching a metro, friends meeting for coffee, or tourists pausing to take in the sights. The area is surrounded by some of Athens' most iconic hotels, such as the Hotel Grande Bretagne, which has hosted countless dignitaries and celebrities since its opening in 1874. Its rooftop restaurant offers stunning views of the Acropolis, making it a favorite spot for visitors.

The square is also a gateway to some of Athens' best shopping and dining experiences. The bustling Ermou Street, one of the city's main commercial thoroughfares, begins at Syntagma Square and stretches westward, lined with a mix of high-end boutiques, international brands, and local shops. For those seeking traditional Greek flavors, nearby tavernas and bakeries serve dishes and pastries that capture the essence of Athens' culinary heritage. Syntagma's central location makes it an ideal starting point for exploring the city, with many major landmarks within walking distance.

The fountains and shaded benches in the square provide a welcome respite for those looking to relax and people-watch. Street performers, artists, and musicians often add to the lively atmosphere, creating a sense of spontaneity and celebration. The square's vibrant energy is balanced by its historical weight, offering a unique space where the layers of Athens' identity come together.

Syntagma Square is also a place of civic engagement, having played a central role in many of Greece's most significant political events. From the constitutional revolution of 1843 to modern-day protests and celebrations, the square has long been a stage for the expression of public sentiment. Its location at the crossroads of Athens' past and present makes it a powerful symbol of the city's resilience and adaptability.

For first-time visitors, the experience of Syntagma Square and the Changing of the Guard is both enlightening and unforgettable. It is a chance to witness living history, to connect with the traditions that have shaped Greece, and to gain a deeper understanding of what makes Athens a city unlike any other. The square is more than just a physical space; it is a reflection of the city's soul, a place where the echoes of the past resonate in the pulse of the present.

Modern Athens: Rooftop Bars and Local Markets

Modern Athens is a city that pulses with life, where ancient history meets a vibrant contemporary scene. While its ruins and historical landmarks often steal the spotlight, the city is equally known for its dynamic modern culture, exemplified by its rooftop bars and bustling local markets. These two facets of urban life reveal a side of Athens that is creative, energetic, and undeniably cosmopolitan, offering visitors a chance to experience the city as its locals do. From panoramic views under the stars to the colorful chaos of market stalls, modern Athens provides countless opportunities to engage with its living, breathing soul.

The rooftop bar culture in Athens has flourished in recent years, becoming a hallmark of the city's nightlife and social scene. With its awe-inspiring skyline dominated by the Acropolis, Athens provides a setting like no other for rooftop venues. These spaces are more than just places for a drink—they are experiences, offering stunning views, creative cocktails, and an atmosphere that captures the city's unique energy. The variety of rooftop bars ensures there's something for everyone, from chic, upscale lounges to relaxed, bohemian hideaways.

One of the most famous rooftop bars in Athens is located atop the Hotel Grande Bretagne, a historic landmark in Syntagma Square. The GB Roof Garden offers an unparalleled view of the Acropolis, particularly magical when illuminated at night. The sophisticated ambiance, paired with expertly crafted cocktails and gourmet dishes, makes it a favorite spot for both locals and visitors seeking an upscale experience. Whether you're sipping on a classic negroni or indulging in a locally inspired cocktail infused with Greek herbs and honey, the surroundings elevate the occasion, blending elegance with a touch of history.

For those looking for a more relaxed vibe, the city has no shortage of casual rooftop options. Bars like A for Athens, located in Monastiraki Square, cater to a younger, more laid-back crowd while still delivering breathtaking views of the Parthenon and the surrounding cityscape. The rooftop is often buzzing with conversation, laughter, and the clinking of glasses, as people gather to soak in the atmosphere. The menu frequently includes local Greek wines, craft beers, and innovative cocktails that incorporate flavors like mastiha, a resin from the island of Chios, or citrus fruits from the Peloponnese. It's a place where the lines between local and tourist blur, as everyone comes together to enjoy the moment.

Athens' rooftop bars aren't limited to views of the Acropolis. Venues like Couleur Locale, also in Monastiraki, provide a more eclectic view of the city, with the Acropolis framed by the urban sprawl that stretches to the horizon. The bar combines industrial-chic décor with a cozy, welcoming atmosphere, offering everything from refreshing spritzes to hearty Greek meze dishes. Nearby, the newer Bios Terrace combines rooftop views with a cultural twist, often hosting art exhibitions, live music, and film screenings alongside its bar offerings. These spaces reflect the creative heartbeat of modern Athens, where art and nightlife blend seamlessly.

While the rooftop bars embody the city's contemporary flair, the local markets reveal its vibrant, everyday life. Athens' markets are a sensory explosion, filled with sights, sounds, and smells that tell the story of its people and their connection to food, tradition, and craftsmanship. The Varvakios Agora, or Central Market, is the beating heart of the city's culinary scene. Located on Athinas Street, this sprawling market is where chefs, home cooks, and curious visitors come to find the freshest ingredients. Its bustling energy is infectious, with vendors calling out their prices, the clang of knives at the butcher stalls, and the vivid colors of produce piled high.

The meat and fish sections of the Varvakios Agora are not for the faint of heart, but they are a fascinating glimpse into the Greek approach to food—fresh, unpretentious, and deeply rooted in tradition. Butchers display everything from lamb and goat to rabbit and poultry, while the fishmongers showcase the day's catch, including octopus, calamari, and sea bream. The produce stalls outside the main hall are a feast for the eyes, offering seasonal fruits and vegetables like figs, citrus, tomatoes, and wild greens. Many of the vendors proudly display signs indicating their produce comes from small farms in regions like Crete, Thessaly, or the Peloponnese, emphasizing the importance of local sourcing in Greek cuisine.

The spice stalls are another highlight of the market, with their heady aromas drawing you in. Here, you can find everything from oregano and thyme to saffron and sumac, as well as blends used in traditional Greek recipes. Olive oils, honey, and cheeses like feta and graviera round out the culinary offerings, providing the perfect opportunity to stock up on authentic Greek flavors. Many vendors are eager to share their knowledge, offering tastings and advice on how to use their products, making the market an interactive and educational experience as well as a shopping destination.

For a more artisanal and eclectic market experience, the Monastiraki Flea Market is a must-visit. Unlike the Varvakios

Agora, which focuses on food, Monastiraki offers an array of goods, from antiques and jewelry to clothing and souvenirs. The narrow streets and alleys of the market are a treasure trove for bargain hunters, with every stall offering something different. Vintage records, handmade leather sandals, traditional evil-eye charms, and secondhand books are just a few of the items you might come across as you wander through the maze of vendors.

Sundays are particularly lively at Monastiraki, as additional vendors set up shop along the streets, creating a festive atmosphere. Live musicians often add to the ambiance, playing everything from rebetiko, a Greek folk music style, to more contemporary tunes. The market's location near key landmarks like the Ancient Agora and the Roman Forum makes it easy to combine a visit with sightseeing, providing a well-rounded day of exploration.

Complementing the flea market is the weekly farmers' markets, or laiki agora, which take place in various neighborhoods throughout Athens. These open-air markets are where locals go to buy their produce, seafood, and other essentials. Visiting a laiki agora offers a more intimate look at Athenian life, as you mingle with residents and experience the rhythms of their daily routines. Vendors take great pride in their goods, often engaging in lively conversations about the quality of their tomatoes or the sweetness of their oranges. The atmosphere is warm and welcoming, reflecting the Greek tradition of hospitality even in the simplest exchanges.

Athens' rooftop bars and local markets may seem like two distinct worlds, but together they paint a complete picture of the city's character. The bars offer a glimpse of its modern, cosmopolitan side, where creativity and innovation thrive, while the markets connect you to its roots, showcasing the traditions and values that have shaped Greek culture for centuries. Both are integral to understanding the essence of Athens, a city that embraces its past while looking boldly toward the future.

Experiencing these facets of modern Athens is not just about seeing the sights or tasting the food; it's about engaging with the city and its people. Whether you're toasting to the view from a rooftop or sampling olives at a market stall, you're participating in the life of Athens, becoming part of its ongoing story. It's a city that invites you to explore, connect, and savor every moment, revealing its essence through the small, everyday joys that make it so unique.

Day Trips from Athens: Delphi, Cape Sounion, and More

Athens, with its vibrant history and dynamic urban landscape, is the perfect launching pad for exploring some of Greece's most remarkable destinations. Just beyond the city's boundaries lie sites of stunning natural beauty, ancient ruins steeped in myth, and charming coastal escapes that offer a refreshing change of pace from the city's bustling streets. Day trips from Athens allow visitors to uncover the rich diversity of the region while immersing themselves in experiences that range from the spiritual to the awe-inspiring. Whether it's a journey to the ancient oracle at Delphi, a sunset at the Temple of Poseidon in Cape Sounion, or a peaceful retreat to nearby islands, these excursions are windows into the broader cultural and geographical tapestry of Greece.

Set amidst the dramatic slopes of Mount Parnassus, Delphi is one of the most celebrated archaeological sites in the world and a destination that captures the imagination of all who visit. In antiquity, Delphi was considered the center of the world, marked by the sacred omphalos stone. Pilgrims from all corners of Greece and beyond traveled to consult the Oracle of Apollo, seeking divine guidance on matters of war, politics, and personal dilemmas. Today, the allure of Delphi lies not only in its historical significance but in its breathtaking setting, where ancient ruins seem to merge seamlessly with the surrounding mountains and valleys.

The journey from Athens to Delphi takes about two and a half hours by car or bus, winding through picturesque villages and verdant landscapes that set the tone for the adventure ahead. Upon arrival, the first stop is typically the Archaeological Site of Delphi, a UNESCO World Heritage Site that includes the Temple of Apollo, the Athenian Treasury, and the ancient theater. The Temple of Apollo, though partially in ruins, remains an evocative centerpiece. Standing among its weathered columns, it's easy to imagine the grandeur and reverence that once defined this sacred space. Climbing higher, the ancient theater offers sweeping views of the site and the surrounding valley, a vista that has inspired countless visitors over the centuries.

The nearby Archaeological Museum of Delphi houses an extraordinary collection of artifacts uncovered at the site, including the famous Charioteer of Delphi, a bronze statue that epitomizes the finesse of ancient Greek artistry. After exploring the ruins and museum, many visitors take time to enjoy the town of Delphi itself, a charming village with traditional tavernas and shops offering local crafts and delicacies. The combination of history, natural beauty, and small-town charm makes a day trip to Delphi an unforgettable experience.

Closer to Athens, Cape Sounion offers a completely different yet equally captivating adventure. Located at the southernmost tip of the Attica peninsula, about an hour and a half from the city, Cape Sounion is renowned for its stunning coastal views and the iconic Temple of Poseidon. The journey to Cape Sounion is a highlight in itself, following the scenic Athenian Riviera along a coastline dotted with beaches, marinas, and seaside villages. The sparkling waters of the Saronic Gulf provide a constant backdrop, inviting travelers to pause and take in the beauty of the Mediterranean.

The Temple of Poseidon, perched on a cliff overlooking the sea, is one of the most striking landmarks in Greece. Built in the 5th century BCE, this Doric temple was dedicated to Poseidon, the god of the sea, a fitting tribute given its dramatic location. The temple's marble columns, though weathered by time, still stand as a testament to the architectural brilliance of ancient Greece. Sunset at Cape Sounion is a particularly magical time to visit, as the golden light bathes the temple and the sea in a warm glow, creating an atmosphere of serenity and wonder. Many visitors choose to stay for dinner at one of the nearby seafood tavernas, savoring freshly caught fish while reflecting on the timeless beauty of the site.

For those seeking island adventures without venturing too far from Athens, the Saronic Gulf islands provide the perfect solution. Aegina, Hydra, and Poros are among the most popular choices, each offering its own unique charm. Aegina, the closest island to Athens, is known for its pistachio orchards, neoclassical architecture, and the impressive Temple of Aphaia. A short ferry ride transports visitors from the bustling port of Piraeus to this tranquil island, where a leisurely pace of life prevails.

Hydra, on the other hand, exudes an air of sophistication and artistic flair. With its car-free streets, stone mansions, and vibrant arts scene, Hydra has long been a haven for writers, painters, and musicians. Visitors can explore the island's cobbled lanes, relax at waterfront cafés, or take a dip in the crystal-clear waters. Poros, with its lush pine forests and picturesque harbor, offers a mix of natural beauty and cultural attractions, including a clock tower that provides panoramic views of the island and the surrounding sea.

The Peloponnese peninsula, located just across the Corinth Canal, is another fantastic option for a day trip from Athens. The ancient city of Corinth, with its impressive archaeological site and museum, is a popular first stop. Here, visitors can explore the Temple of Apollo, the ancient agora, and the Acrocorinth, a fortified hilltop that offers commanding views of the Corinthian Gulf. Further afield, the theater of Epidaurus and the ruins of Mycenae provide additional opportunities to delve into Greece's storied past.

For nature enthusiasts, the Mount Parnitha National Park, just a short drive from Athens, offers a peaceful retreat into the wilderness. The park is home to a diverse range of flora and fauna, as well as hiking trails that lead to breathtaking vistas, caves, and springs. Whether you're an experienced hiker or simply looking for a leisurely walk in nature, Mount Parnitha provides a refreshing escape from the urban environment.

Each of these day trips from Athens offers something unique, allowing visitors to experience the diverse landscapes and cultural heritage of the region. Whether you're drawn to the mystical aura of Delphi, the coastal splendor of Cape Sounion, the charm of the Saronic islands, or the historical treasures of the Peloponnese, these excursions enrich your understanding of Greece and its enduring allure. Athens may be the starting point, but the adventures beyond its borders are equally integral to discovering the essence of this extraordinary country.

CHAPTER 3: THE GREEK ISLANDS – PARADISE ON EARTH

A Guide to the Cyclades: Santorini, Mykonos, and Naxos

The Cyclades archipelago is the epitome of Greek island beauty, a cluster of over 200 islands scattered across the azure waters of the Aegean Sea. Among them, Santorini, Mykonos, and Naxos stand as jewels, each offering its distinct charm, character, and allure. Whether you're drawn to breathtaking sunsets, vibrant nightlife, or serene landscapes steeped in history, these islands provide a diverse range of experiences that captivate travelers from across the globe. Exploring the Cyclades is not just about visiting islands; it's about immersing yourself in the essence of Greek culture, blending natural beauty with centuries-old traditions.

Santorini, perhaps the most iconic of the Cyclades, is a destination that often feels like stepping into a postcard. Its dramatic landscape, shaped by a massive volcanic eruption thousands of years ago, sets it apart from the other islands. The caldera, a sunken volcanic crater now filled with the shimmering blue of the Aegean, provides a breathtaking backdrop to the whitewashed villages that cling to its cliffs. Fira, the island's capital, offers a lively mix of shops, restaurants, and bars, all perched precariously above the caldera. Walking through its narrow cobblestone streets, you're treated to stunning views at every turn, while the scent of fresh seafood and local specialties wafts through the air.

Oia, located on the northern tip of Santorini, is synonymous with the island's famous sunsets. Visitors and locals alike gather in this picturesque village each evening, finding their spot along the cliffs or on the terraces of quaint cafés to watch the sun dip below the horizon. The sky transforms into a canvas of warm hues—deep orange, fiery red, and soft pink—casting a magical glow over the caldera. Oia's charm extends beyond its sunsets, with its elegant boutique hotels, art galleries, and the iconic blue-domed churches that dot the landscape.

Santorini's volcanic origins have blessed the island with unique beaches, each offering its own distinct character. The Red Beach, named for the striking red cliffs that tower above its shores, feels almost otherworldly, while the black sand beaches of Perissa and Kamari are perfect for sunbathing and swimming. For those seeking a deeper connection to the island's history, the ancient ruins of Akrotiri offer a fascinating glimpse into a Minoan settlement preserved by volcanic ash. Often referred to as the "Pompeii of the Aegean," Akrotiri provides insight into the advanced civilization that once thrived here, with its sophisticated architecture, frescoes, and artifacts.

While Santorini captivates with its dramatic beauty, Mykonos exudes a vibrant energy that has made it one of the most famous party destinations in the world. Known as the "Island of the Winds," Mykonos combines cosmopolitan glamour with traditional charm, attracting a diverse crowd of celebrities, jet-setters, and travelers seeking unforgettable experiences. Mykonos Town, or Chora, is the island's beating heart, a maze of whitewashed alleys lined with stylish boutiques, chic bars, and upscale restaurants. The town's design, with its winding streets and hidden corners, was originally intended to confuse pirates, but today it adds an element of discovery to every visit.

One of Mykonos' most iconic landmarks is the row of 16th-century windmills overlooking the harbor. These windmills, once used to grind grain, now stand as a symbol of the island's heritage and provide a stunning backdrop for photos. Nearby, the neighborhood of Little Venice enchants visitors with its colorful waterfront buildings, many of which house lively bars and restaurants. Sitting at a table by the water, you can enjoy a cocktail or a plate of fresh seafood as the waves lap against the shore, creating a romantic and unforgettable atmosphere.

The beaches of Mykonos are legendary, offering a mix of relaxation and revelry to suit every mood. Paradise and Super Paradise beaches are the epicenters of the island's party scene, with beach clubs pumping music from afternoon until dawn. For a more tranquil experience, Elia Beach and Agios Sostis provide serene stretches of sand and crystal-clear waters, perfect for unwinding. Mykonos also offers opportunities for exploration beyond its beaches and nightlife. The island is home to the ancient site of Delos, a short boat ride away. Delos, considered the birthplace of Apollo and Artemis in Greek mythology, is a UNESCO World Heritage Site with well-preserved ruins that tell the story of its importance as a cultural and religious center in antiquity.

Naxos, the largest of the Cyclades, offers a completely different experience, one that is defined by its lush landscapes, traditional villages, and rich history. Unlike the cosmopolitan buzz of Mykonos or the dramatic vistas of Santorini, Naxos is an island that invites you to slow down and connect with its serene beauty. The island's main town, also called Naxos or Chora, greets visitors with its charming harbor and the iconic Portara, a massive marble doorway that is all that remains of a temple dedicated to Apollo. Standing on the small islet of Palatia and connected to the main island by a causeway, the Portara is a striking symbol of Naxos and a favorite spot for watching the sunset.

Chora itself is a delightful blend of medieval and Cycladic architecture, with its Venetian castle, narrow alleys, and whitewashed houses. The Kastro, or castle district, offers a glimpse into the island's Venetian past, with its mansions, churches, and cultural institutions such as the Archaeological Museum of Naxos. The museum's collection includes artifacts from the Cycladic civilization and beyond, providing a deeper understanding of the island's historical significance.

Naxos' interior is a patchwork of fertile valleys, rugged mountains, and picturesque villages, each with its own unique character. Villages such as Apiranthos, Halki, and Filoti invite you to wander their cobbled streets, sample local delicacies, and meet the warm and welcoming residents. The island's agricultural heritage is evident in its cuisine, which features ingredients like potatoes, cheeses, and citrus fruits grown in its fertile soil. A visit to a local tavern is a must, where you can savor dishes like kitron, a liqueur made from citron fruit, or graviera cheese, a Naxian specialty.

Naxos is also a paradise for outdoor enthusiasts, with its hiking trails, windsurfing spots, and pristine beaches. Agios

Prokopios and Plaka are among the island's most popular beaches, offering long stretches of golden sand and calm, turquoise waters. For those seeking adventure, the hiking trails that wind through the island's mountains and valleys reveal hidden gems, from ancient ruins to secluded chapels and breathtaking vistas.

Each of these islands—Santorini, Mykonos, and Naxos—offers a distinct experience, yet together they embody the essence of the Cyclades. Santorini enchants with its dramatic beauty and timeless allure, Mykonos dazzles with its vibrant energy and cosmopolitan flair, and Naxos captivates with its authenticity and natural charm. Exploring these islands is not just about ticking off destinations; it's about embracing the diversity and richness of Greek island life. Whether you find yourself gazing at a caldera sunset, dancing until dawn, or savoring a quiet moment in a mountain village, the Cyclades leave an indelible mark on your heart and soul.

Crete: Beaches, Mountains, and Minoan History

Crete, the largest of the Greek islands, stretches out like a world of its own, offering a captivating blend of pristine beaches, rugged mountains, and ancient history that dates back to the dawn of European civilization. The island's diverse landscape, combined with its rich cultural heritage and warm hospitality, makes it a destination that appeals to every kind of traveler. From the turquoise waters of its coastlines to the dramatic peaks of the White Mountains, and from the remnants of the Minoan civilization to picturesque villages where time seems to stand still, Crete is a tapestry of wonders waiting to be explored.

The beaches of Crete are among the most stunning in the Mediterranean, each with its own unique character and charm. Along the western coast, Elafonissi Beach stands out as a true paradise. Known for its pink-hued sands and shallow, crystalline waters, this beach feels like something out of a dream. The sand gets its blush color from crushed seashells, adding to the surreal beauty of the setting. Elafonissi is not just a beach—it's also a protected area of natural significance, with sand dunes, rare plants, and a lagoon that attracts migratory birds. Visitors often spend hours wading through the shallow waters or simply lounging under the sun, marveling at the tranquility of the surroundings.

Further north, Balos Lagoon offers a breathtaking scene that is both wild and serene. Accessible via a hike or a short boat ride, Balos is a stunning combination of white sand, turquoise waters, and rugged cliffs. The lagoon's shallow waters are perfect for swimming, while the panoramic views from the cliffs above are nothing short of spectacular. Balos is a place where nature reigns supreme, and its untouched beauty leaves a lasting impression on all who visit.

On the eastern side of the island, Vai Beach presents a completely different but equally captivating experience. Surrounded by Europe's largest natural palm forest, Vai feels like an exotic escape. The golden sands and clear waters provide the perfect setting for relaxation, while the swaying palm trees create an atmosphere of tropical bliss. Vai's uniqueness lies in its striking contrast to the rugged terrain that dominates much of Crete, offering a glimpse into the island's incredible diversity.

Beyond its beaches, Crete's mountainous interior is a haven for adventurers and nature lovers. The White Mountains, or Lefka Ori, dominate the western region and are home to some of the most dramatic landscapes on the island. Samaria Gorge, a 16-kilometer-long canyon that cuts through the heart of the mountains, is a must-visit for hikers. The trail begins at the Omalos Plateau and descends through a series of breathtaking landscapes, from towering cliffs to shaded woodlands and narrow passes. The gorge culminates at the village of Agia Roumeli, where hikers are rewarded with a refreshing swim in the Libyan Sea. The experience of traversing Samaria Gorge is both physically challenging and immensely rewarding, offering a sense of connection to Crete's untamed beauty.

The Psiloritis Range, also known as Mount Ida, is another highlight of Crete's mountainous terrain. As the highest peak on the island, Psiloritis holds a significant place in Greek mythology—it is said to be the birthplace of Zeus, the king of the gods. The Ideon Cave, located on the slopes of the mountain, is believed to be the site where Zeus was hidden and raised by the nymph Amalthea. Today, the cave is a popular destination for those interested in mythology and archaeology, as well as for those seeking to immerse themselves in the mystical aura of the place.

Crete's mountains are also home to traditional villages that offer a glimpse into the island's authentic way of life. Villages like Anogeia, Zaros, and Spili are known for their warm hospitality, traditional architecture, and local crafts. In

Anogeia, visitors can witness the art of weaving and embroidery, while Zaros is famous for its freshwater springs and delicious trout. Spili, with its Venetian-style fountains and vibrant flowers, is a picture-perfect stop where you can enjoy a leisurely stroll and sample local delicacies like honey and raki.

No visit to Crete would be complete without delving into its ancient history, which is deeply intertwined with the rise of the Minoan civilization. The Minoans, who flourished on the island between 2000 and 1400 BCE, are considered one of the earliest advanced civilizations in Europe. Their legacy is most vividly preserved at the Palace of Knossos, located near Heraklion. This sprawling archaeological site, often referred to as Europe's oldest city, was the political and cultural center of Minoan Crete.

The Palace of Knossos is a labyrinthine complex of courtyards, corridors, and chambers, reflecting the sophistication and ingenuity of the Minoans. The site's colorful frescoes, depicting scenes of nature, ritual, and daily life, provide a window into the vibrant culture that once thrived here. One of the most famous images is that of the bull-leaping fresco, which portrays an athletic ritual that may have held religious significance. The legend of the Minotaur and the Labyrinth, immortalized in Greek mythology, is often associated with Knossos, adding an air of mystery to the site.

Other significant Minoan sites on the island include Phaistos, Malia, and Zakros. The Palace of Phaistos, perched on a hill overlooking the fertile Messara Plain, offers stunning views alongside its historical significance. The Phaistos Disc, a unique artifact inscribed with undeciphered symbols, was discovered here and remains one of archaeology's great mysteries. Malia, located near the northern coast, is known for its impressive storage magazines and ceremonial areas, while Zakros, on the eastern edge of the island, is the smallest of the major Minoan palaces but no less fascinating.

Crete's history extends beyond the Minoans, with influences from the Romans, Byzantines, Venetians, and Ottomans leaving their mark on the island. The Venetian harbor of Chania, with its lighthouse and colorful buildings, is a testament to this layered history. The old town of Rethymno, with its narrow alleys and historic fort, offers a similar blend of architectural styles and cultural influences. These towns are not only beautiful but also serve as living museums, where the past and present coexist seamlessly.

Cretan cuisine is another integral part of the island's identity, rooted in its agricultural heritage and Mediterranean traditions. The island is known for its fresh ingredients, from olive oil and wild herbs to honey and cheese. Dishes like dakos—a barley rusk topped with tomatoes, feta, and olive oil—and kalitsounia, sweet or savory pastries, showcase the simplicity and flavor of Cretan cooking. Dining at a traditional taverna, where recipes are passed down through generations, is an experience that connects you to the heart of Crete.

The people of Crete are known for their hospitality, or "philoxenia," a concept deeply ingrained in Greek culture. Whether you're greeted with a warm smile in a village square or offered a shot of raki after a meal, the Cretans' genuine kindness and generosity leave a lasting impression. This sense of connection, combined with the island's natural beauty and historical depth, makes Crete a destination that resonates on a profound level.

Crete is a land of contrasts, where mountains meet the sea, and ancient history intertwines with modern life. Its beaches, mountains, and Minoan sites offer a diverse range of experiences that cater to every interest, while its warm people and rich culture create a sense of belonging that stays with you long after you've left. Exploring Crete is not just a journey through a remarkable island but a journey through the essence of Greece itself.

The Dodecanese Islands: Rhodes and Kos

Rhodes and Kos, two of the most prominent islands in the Dodecanese archipelago, offer a captivating blend of history, culture, and natural beauty. This southeastern corner of Greece, close to the shores of Turkey, is steeped in a unique mix of influences that have shaped its identity over centuries. From ancient ruins that whisper tales of bygone eras to medieval fortresses standing as symbols of resilience, and from lively towns to serene beaches, these islands promise an experience that is as diverse as it is enriching. Exploring Rhodes and Kos is not merely a journey across beautiful landscapes but also an immersion into layers of history and tradition that set them apart from other Greek islands.

Rhodes, often referred to as the "Island of the Knights," is a destination that immediately captures the imagination. Its most iconic feature is the medieval Old Town, a UNESCO World Heritage Site that feels like stepping into a time machine. Enclosed within massive stone walls, this historic quarter is a labyrinth of cobblestone streets, ancient buildings, and hidden courtyards. Every corner seems to tell a story, with the legacy of the Knights of St. John—a military and religious order that ruled the island from the 14th to the 16th century—woven into the very fabric of the city. The Palace of the Grand Master is the crown jewel of the Old Town, an imposing fortress-palace that dominates the skyline. Inside, visitors can wander through halls adorned with mosaics, medieval artifacts, and Gothic architecture, all of which reflect the grandeur and power of the knights who once called this place home.

The Street of the Knights, a perfectly preserved medieval pathway, is another highlight of Rhodes' Old Town. Flanked by grand stone buildings that once served as inns for the knights, each representing a different "tongue" or nationality within the order, this street is a testament to the island's cosmopolitan past. As you walk along its length, it's impossible not to feel a sense of awe at the history that unfolded here. Beyond the Old Town, the modern city of Rhodes offers a lively atmosphere with its waterfront cafés, bustling markets, and a vibrant nightlife, providing a sharp yet complementary contrast to the historical core.

Rhodes is also home to ancient ruins that predate the medieval era by millennia. The Acropolis of Lindos, perched high above the picturesque village of the same name, is a site of extraordinary beauty and significance. The journey to the top involves a climb along winding paths lined with whitewashed houses, but the reward is well worth the effort. The view from the acropolis is breathtaking, with the Aegean

Sea stretching endlessly in every direction and St. Paul's Bay shimmering below. The ruins themselves include a temple dedicated to Athena Lindia, dating back to the 4th century BCE, as well as Hellenistic and Roman structures that add to the site's historical richness.

For those seeking relaxation, Rhodes boasts some of the most beautiful beaches in the Dodecanese. Faliraki Beach, with its golden sands and crystal-clear waters, is perfect for families and those looking for convenience, as it is lined with restaurants, bars, and water sports facilities. For a more tranquil escape, Tsambika Beach offers a serene setting surrounded by rugged hills, while Prasonisi, located at the southern tip of the island, is a haven for windsurfers and kiteboarders. The diversity of Rhodes' coastline ensures there's a spot for every type of traveler, whether you prefer bustling resorts or hidden coves.

Moving on to Kos, the island offers an entirely different yet equally compelling experience. Known as the "Island of Hippocrates," Kos carries the legacy of the ancient physician who is often regarded as the father of medicine. This connection to Hippocrates is most evident at the Asklepion, an ancient healing sanctuary dedicated to Asclepius, the god of medicine. Situated on a hillside overlooking the sea, the Asklepion is a place of immense historical and spiritual significance. The terraced ruins include temples, treatment rooms, and a Roman bath complex, all of which give insight into the advanced medical practices of the ancient Greeks. Standing amidst these remnants, it's easy to imagine the pilgrims who once traveled here seeking cures and guidance.

The town of Kos, the island's main hub, is a lively blend of ancient and modern elements. Its centerpiece is the Tree of Hippocrates, under which the physician is said to have taught his students. While the current tree is a descendant of the original, its presence serves as a powerful symbol of Kos' historical identity. Nearby, the ruins of the ancient agora and the medieval Castle of the Knights provide further opportunities to delve into the island's storied past. The castle, strategically located at the entrance to the harbor, is a reminder of Kos' importance as a defensive stronghold during the era of the Knights of St. John.

Kos is also renowned for its stunning natural landscapes and beaches. Paradise Beach, true to its name, is a slice of heaven with its powdery sand and turquoise waters. It's an ideal spot for swimming, sunbathing, or simply soaking in the beauty of the surroundings. Kefalos Beach, located near the village of the same name, offers a more laid-back atmosphere and is popular among windsurfers. For a unique experience, visitors can explore the thermal springs at Therma Beach, where warm, mineral-rich waters flow into the sea, creating a natural spa environment.

Beyond its beaches, Kos is dotted with charming villages that provide a glimpse into the island's traditional way of life. Zia, nestled in the mountains, is a favorite among visitors for its panoramic views and vibrant sunsets. The village's narrow streets are lined with shops selling handmade crafts, local honey, and herbs, while its tavernas serve authentic Cretan dishes that highlight the island's culinary heritage. Kardamena and Tigaki, though more developed, retain their charm and are excellent bases for exploring the island's attractions.

What sets the Dodecanese islands apart is their rich tapestry of influences, which is evident in every aspect of life on Rhodes and Kos. From the Venetian and Ottoman architecture to the fusion of flavors in the local cuisine, these islands are a testament to their complex history as crossroads of culture and commerce. Meze dishes like dolmades, tzatziki, and grilled octopus are staples, while desserts such as baklava and loukoumades reflect the islands' ties to the broader Mediterranean and Middle Eastern worlds. Dining on fresh seafood at a seaside taverna, with the waves gently lapping against the shore, is an experience that encapsulates the essence of island life.

The people of Rhodes and Kos are known for their warmth and hospitality, making visitors feel like part of the community. Whether it's a shopkeeper offering a taste of local olive oil or a taverna owner sharing stories about the island's history, these interactions add depth and authenticity to the travel experience. The rhythm of life on these islands is both invigorating and soothing, inviting you to explore at your own pace while savoring every moment.

Rhodes and Kos are more than just destinations—they are gateways to understanding the enduring allure of the Dodecanese. Each island offers a distinct blend of historical intrigue, natural beauty, and cultural richness, yet together they paint a cohesive picture of a region that has captivated travelers for centuries. Whether you're wandering through the medieval streets of Rhodes, standing in awe at the Asklepion of Kos, or simply basking in the sun on a pristine beach, the Dodecanese islands leave an indelible mark on your soul.

Ionian Islands: Corfu, Zakynthos, and Kefalonia

The Ionian Islands, strung like a jeweled necklace along Greece's western coast, are a region of unparalleled beauty, where emerald-green waters meet dramatic cliffs, verdant hillsides, and charming villages. Among these islands, Corfu, Zakynthos, and Kefalonia stand out as destinations that each carry their own distinct allure. Whether it's the Venetian elegance of Corfu, the stunning beaches of Zakynthos, or Kefalonia's raw natural splendor, the Ionian Islands weave together a narrative of relaxation, exploration, and timeless charm. These islands embody the perfect balance of history, culture, and breathtaking landscapes, making them an essential part of any journey to Greece.

Corfu, often referred to as the "Emerald Isle," is a place where history and nature intertwine seamlessly. The island's capital, Corfu Town, is a UNESCO World Heritage Site and a masterpiece of Venetian, French, and British influences. Walking through its cobblestone streets, you're enveloped by the charm of pastel-colored buildings, wrought-iron balconies, and bougainvillea-draped façades. The Spianada Square, one of the largest in Europe, is a lively hub surrounded by cafés, where locals and visitors alike gather to soak in the atmosphere. The Liston Arcade, with its elegant archways, is a nod to Corfu's French history, inspired by the Rue de Rivoli in Paris. Sitting here with a cup of Greek coffee, watching the world go by, feels like stepping into a more refined, timeless era.

Corfu's Old Fortress and New Fortress are imposing landmarks that tell the story of the island's strategic importance throughout history. The Old Fortress, built by the Venetians, offers panoramic views of the town and the shimmering Ionian Sea. Exploring its bastions and tunnels, you can almost hear the echoes of battles fought long ago. Nearby, the New Fortress is equally impressive, a testament to Corfu's role as a stronghold against Ottoman invasions. These historical sites offer more than just a glimpse into the island's past—they provide a sense of its resilience and enduring spirit.

Beyond Corfu Town, the island is a paradise of lush landscapes and idyllic beaches. Paleokastritsa, on the island's western coast, is a must-visit for its stunning bays and crystal-clear waters framed by olive groves and towering cliffs. Legend has it that this was the site of Odysseus's last stop before returning home, adding a layer of myth to its already enchanting scenery. Nearby, the monastery of Theotokos sits atop a hill, offering not only spiritual solace but also breathtaking views of the coastline. For a more secluded experience, Rovinia Beach, accessible only by foot or boat, is a hidden gem where you can escape the crowds and immerse yourself in nature's tranquility.

Zakynthos, or Zante as it's often called, is an island that dazzles with its striking contrasts. Its most famous landmark, Navagio Beach—commonly known as Shipwreck Beach—is a sight that defies imagination. Enclosed by towering limestone cliffs and accessible only by boat, the beach gets its name from the wreck of the MV Panagiotis, which lies half-buried in its white sands. The azure waters here are so vibrant they almost seem unreal, making it one of the most photographed spots in Greece. Visiting Navagio is a surreal experience, whether you're standing on the cliffside viewpoint above or feeling the sand beneath your toes on the beach itself.

The Blue Caves, located along Zakynthos' northern coast, are another of the island's natural marvels. These sea caves, carved into the cliffs by centuries of waves, are a playground for light and water. As sunlight filters through the openings, the water glows an otherworldly shade of blue, creating an unforgettable visual spectacle. Boat tours often include stops for swimming and snorkeling, allowing you to fully embrace the magic of this underwater wonderland.

Zakynthos is also known for its role in marine conservation, particularly as a nesting site for the endangered loggerhead sea turtle, or Caretta caretta. The beaches of Laganas Bay, part of the Zakynthos Marine Park, are protected areas where these turtles come to lay their eggs. Visiting these beaches offers a chance to witness nature's delicate balance while supporting efforts to preserve this vital habitat. Guided tours, led by local conservationists, provide insights into the turtles' life cycle and the importance of protecting them for future generations.

Away from its beaches, Zakynthos reveals a quieter, more traditional side. The village of Keri, perched on a hill overlooking the sea, is a place where time seems to slow down. Its stone houses, narrow streets, and family-run tavernas offer a taste of authentic island life. From the Keri Lighthouse, you can enjoy one of the most breathtaking sunsets in the Ionian, as the sun dips below the horizon and paints the sky in hues of gold and crimson.

Kefalonia, the largest of the Ionian Islands, is a land of dramatic landscapes and unspoiled beauty. The island's rugged terrain is dominated by Mount Ainos, a national park covered in rare fir trees that are unique to the region. Hiking trails lead to panoramic viewpoints where you can take in the island's diverse scenery, from its rocky cliffs to its lush valleys. The park is also home to wild horses, adding an element of surprise to your exploration.

Myrtos Beach, often ranked among the most beautiful in the world, is one of Kefalonia's crown jewels. Nestled between steep cliffs, its white pebble shore and turquoise waters create a scene of unparalleled beauty. The beach's remote location and lack of overdevelopment make it feel like a slice of paradise untouched by time. For those who prefer a more secluded setting, Antisamos Beach, near the village of Sami, offers a similar allure with its verdant backdrop and calm waters.

Kefalonia's charm extends beyond its natural wonders to its villages and towns. Assos, a tiny village set on a peninsula, is a postcard-perfect destination with its colorful houses and Venetian castle. The village's tranquil harbor is the ideal place to enjoy fresh seafood while taking in the serene surroundings. Fiskardo, located on the island's northern tip, is another gem, known for its well-preserved architecture and cosmopolitan vibe. Once a refuge for the wealthy during the Venetian era, Fiskardo retains an air of elegance that sets it apart from other island towns.

The island's subterranean treasures are equally impressive. The Melissani Cave, a partially submerged cavern with an underground lake, is a natural wonder that captivates all who visit. As sunlight filters through the cave's opening, the water takes on an ethereal blue hue, creating a dreamy, almost magical atmosphere. Nearby, the Drogarati Cave boasts impressive stalactites and stalagmites, offering a glimpse into the island's geological history.

Cultural influences on the Ionian Islands are distinctly different from those in the Aegean, reflecting centuries of Venetian, French, and British rule. This is evident in everything from the architecture to the cuisine. Dishes like pastitsada, a hearty pasta dish with a Venetian twist, and sofrito, a slow-cooked beef dish, are staples of Corfu's culinary scene. Zakynthos offers its own delights, including ladotyri, a local cheese aged in olive oil, while Kefalonia is known for its wine, particularly the Robola grape, which produces crisp, aromatic whites. Dining in the Ionian Islands is an experience that engages all the senses, with fresh ingredients and traditional recipes that reflect the islands' rich heritage.

The Ionian Islands' allure lies not only in their physical beauty but also in the stories they tell. From Corfu's Venetian past to Zakynthos' commitment to marine conservation and Kefalonia's geological wonders, these islands offer a tapestry of experiences that are as enriching as they are unforgettable. Whether you're exploring ancient fortresses, diving into crystal-clear waters, or simply savoring a meal at a seaside taverna, the Ionian Islands leave an indelible mark on your soul, a reminder of the timeless magic that Greece has to offer.

CHAPTER 4: ANCIENT GREECE – MYTHOLOGY AND HISTORY COME TO LIFE

The Gods and Myths That Shaped a Civilization

Greek mythology, a cornerstone of Western civilization, is a vast and interconnected tapestry of gods, heroes, myths, and legends that shaped the cultural, spiritual, and political identity of ancient Greece. These myths, passed down orally for centuries before being preserved in written form, were not just stories but profound reflections of the human condition, natural phenomena, and the mysteries of existence. They provided explanations for the inexplicable, moral lessons for society, and a framework for understanding the divine. The pantheon of gods and the myths surrounding them influenced every aspect of Greek life, from religion and politics to art, literature, and philosophy, leaving an indelible mark on history.

At the heart of Greek mythology was Mount Olympus, the mythical home of the Olympian gods. Perched high above the mortal world, Olympus was imagined as a place of eternal splendor, where the gods lived in harmony—though not without conflict, for even the gods were subject to their own passions and flaws. Zeus, the king of the gods, ruled over Olympus with his mighty thunderbolt, embodying the ideals of authority and justice. Yet, Zeus was far from perfect. His numerous affairs and the resulting offspring were central to countless myths, illustrating the gods' complex relationships with both mortals and each other. His reign was marked by a delicate balance of power, often tested by challenges from within Olympus and beyond.

Hera, Zeus's wife and queen of the gods, was the goddess of marriage and family. She was known for her fierce jealousy and her relentless pursuit of vengeance against Zeus's lovers and illegitimate children. Hera's myths, while often tragic, reveal the ancient Greeks' perspectives on loyalty, betrayal, and the struggles within relationships. Her rivalry with figures such as Leto, Semele, and Heracles (one of Zeus's many children) underscores the tensions that defined the divine realm, mirroring the complexities of human life.

Poseidon, the god of the sea, earthquakes, and horses, was another central figure in the Greek pantheon. His domain, the vast and unpredictable ocean, reflected his own tempestuous nature. Poseidon's myths often depict his contentious relationships with both mortals and gods. His feud with Athena over the patronage of Athens, for example, led to the creation of the olive tree, a symbol of peace and prosperity. This myth not only highlights Poseidon's volatile temperament but also underscores the importance of competition and innovation in Greek culture.

Athena, the goddess of wisdom, strategy, and warfare, was one of the most revered deities in ancient Greece. Born fully grown and armored from Zeus's forehead, she embodied the ideals of intelligence and rationality. Athena's myths often showcase her role as a protector and guide, such as her assistance to Odysseus in the Odyssey and her mentorship of Perseus in his quest to slay Medusa. Her virginity, a symbol of her independence, set her apart from other goddesses, emphasizing her unique position within the pantheon.

Apollo and Artemis, twin children of Zeus and Leto, represented the duality of light and darkness, order and chaos. Apollo, the god of music, prophecy, and healing, was associated with reason and harmony. His oracle at Delphi was one of the most significant religious sites in ancient Greece, where mortals sought divine guidance. Artemis, the goddess of the hunt and wilderness, was a fierce protector of nature and a symbol of untamed freedom. Together, the twins encapsulated the balance of opposites that was central to Greek thought.

Aphrodite, the goddess of love and beauty, was both enchanting and formidable. Born from the sea foam, she wielded immense power over gods and mortals alike through her ability to inspire desire. Her relationships, notably with Ares, the god of war, and Hephaestus, the god of craftsmanship, reveal the interconnectedness of love, conflict, and creation. Aphrodite's influence extended beyond romance, shaping myths that explored themes of jealousy, betrayal, and the consequences of unchecked passion.

The underworld, ruled by Hades, was a realm of mystery and fear. Unlike the Christian concept of hell, the Greek underworld was not a place of punishment but a shadowy domain where all souls eventually resided. Hades, though often portrayed as stern and unyielding, was not inherently malevolent. His abduction of Persephone, which led to the changing seasons, is one of the most poignant myths in Greek mythology. The story illustrates the cycle of life and death, the inevitability of change, and the enduring bond between mother and daughter.

The myths of the gods were deeply intertwined with the lives of mortals, who often found themselves at the mercy of divine whims. Heroes such as Heracles, Theseus, and Perseus bridged the gap between gods and humans, undertaking extraordinary feats that tested their strength, courage, and morality. Heracles, the son of Zeus and a mortal woman, was tasked with completing twelve labors as penance for a crime committed in a fit of madness inflicted by Hera. These labors, which included slaying the Nemean Lion and capturing the Golden Hind of Artemis, symbolized the human struggle against insurmountable odds and the quest for redemption.

The Trojan War, one of the most famous events in Greek mythology, was a grand tapestry woven with the threads of divine intervention, human ambition, and tragic fate. Sparked by the abduction of Helen by Paris, the war brought together legendary figures such as Achilles, Hector, and Odysseus. The gods played an active role in the conflict, taking sides and influencing its outcome. The Iliad and the Odyssey, attributed to Homer, immortalized these events, blending history and mythology into epic narratives that continue to resonate.

Greek mythology also sought to explain natural phenomena and the origins of the world. The creation myth, as recounted in Hesiod's Theogony, begins with Chaos, a primordial void from which the first deities emerged. Gaia, the personification of the Earth, and Uranus, the sky, gave birth to the Titans, who were eventually overthrown by the Olympians. This cycle of creation and destruction reflects the Greeks' understanding of the universe as a dynamic and ever-changing entity.

The myths were not static; they evolved over time, adapting to the changing needs and values of Greek society. They were performed in theater, depicted in art, and inscribed in literature, serving as both entertainment and education. The tragedies of Aeschylus, Sophocles, and Euripides brought these myths to life on stage, exploring themes of fate, hubris, and the human condition. Vase paintings, sculptures, and mosaics immortalized the gods and heroes, ensuring their stories would endure.

Greek mythology's influence extends far beyond antiquity. It has shaped Western literature, philosophy, and art, inspiring works from Dante's Divine Comedy to Percy Jackson's modern adventures. The gods and myths of ancient Greece continue to captivate the imagination, offering timeless lessons about humanity's strengths, flaws, and aspirations.

These myths were more than mere stories; they were a framework for understanding the world and humanity's place within it. They offered explanations for the unexplainable, comfort in times of uncertainty, and a sense of connection to something greater. The gods, with all their power and imperfection, reflected the complexities of human nature, making them both relatable and awe-inspiring. Through mythology, the ancient Greeks sought to make sense of their existence, leaving behind a legacy that continues to inspire and enlighten.

Olympia: Birthplace of the Olympic Games

Nestled in the verdant valley of the Alpheios River in the Peloponnese, Olympia is a site of immense historical and cultural significance, revered as the birthplace of the Olympic Games. In ancient Greece, this sanctuary was a center of worship, athletic excellence, and unifying spirit, where warring city-states set aside their differences to honor the gods through competition. Olympia was not just a place of sport; it was a sacred ground where religion, politics, and athletics converged, embodying the ideals of harmony and excellence that defined Greek civilization. Visiting Olympia is an opportunity to step back in time, to walk in the footsteps of athletes, spectators, and priests who gathered here more than two millennia ago.

The origins of the Olympic Games can be traced back to 776 BCE, though the traditions surrounding them are believed to be even older. The games were held in honor of Zeus, the king of the gods, and took place every four years—a tradition that continues to this day in the modern Olympic calendar. The ancient games were much more than an athletic competition; they were a religious festival that brought together participants and spectators from across the Greek world. The Olympic Truce, or ekecheiria, was declared during the games, halting conflicts and ensuring safe passage for athletes and visitors. This gathering of city-states, often at odds with one another, highlighted the unifying power of Olympia.

At the heart of Olympia stood the magnificent Temple of Zeus, one of the Seven Wonders of the Ancient World. This colossal structure, built in the 5th century BCE, housed a statue of Zeus crafted by the renowned sculptor Phidias. The statue, made of gold and ivory, depicted the god seated on a throne, holding a scepter in one hand and a statue of Nike, the goddess of victory, in the other. It was a masterpiece of ancient art and a symbol of divine authority. Although the temple and statue no longer exist, their legacy endures in the cultural memory of Greece and the world.

Nearby, the Temple of Hera, one of the oldest Doric temples in Greece, served as another focal point of Olympia. Dedicated to Zeus's wife, Hera, the temple was the site of significant rituals, including the lighting of the sacred flame. This flame, ignited by the sun's rays using a parabolic mirror, symbolized purity and the divine connection between the gods and humanity. The tradition of the Olympic flame, which begins in Olympia and travels to the host city of the modern games, is a continuation of this ancient practice.

The Altis, or sacred grove, was the spiritual heart of Olympia, a sanctuary that held shrines, altars, and other religious monuments. It was here that the sacred olive tree grew, from which crowns were fashioned for Olympic victors. These crowns, known as kotinos, were the ultimate prize, representing not material wealth but the glory of achievement and the favor of the gods. The Altis was also adorned with countless statues and votive offerings, dedicated by city-states and individuals in gratitude or commemoration.

The athletic events of the ancient games were held in the stadium, a simple yet monumental space that could accommodate up to 45,000 spectators. The stadium, unlike its modern counterparts, was an open field with no seats; spectators sat on the surrounding slopes. The starting and finishing lines, marked by stone blocks, are still visible today, providing a tangible connection to the athletes who once competed there. Events included running races, wrestling, boxing, discus and javelin throwing, long jump, and the pentathlon, which combined five disciplines to test an athlete's versatility.

The hippodrome, located near the stadium, was the venue for chariot and horse races, events that were as thrilling as they were dangerous. Chariot racing, in particular, was a spectacle of speed and skill, with teams of horses pulling lightweight carts around a track at breakneck speeds. These races were often sponsored by wealthy patrons, whose prestige was enhanced by their victories. The charioteer, though the one who risked life and limb, rarely received the glory; it was the owner of the horses who was celebrated.

One of the most fascinating aspects of Olympia is the gymnasium and palaestra, where athletes trained in preparation for the games. The gymnasium, a large rectangular area surrounded by colonnades, was used for running, jumping, and other exercises. The palaestra, a smaller enclosed space, was devoted to wrestling, boxing, and other combat sports. These training facilities were not just physical spaces but centers of education, where athletes were taught discipline, strategy, and the importance of fair play. Coaches and trainers played a crucial role in shaping the skills and character of their protégés, emphasizing the balance between mind and body.

The role of women in ancient Olympia was complex and often contradictory. While the games themselves were an exclusively male domain—both as participants and spectators—women were not entirely excluded from Olympia's cultural life. The Heraia, a separate athletic competition for women, was held in honor of Hera and featured foot races for unmarried girls. These races, although less prominent than the Olympic Games, reflected the evolving place of women in Greek society. The priestesses of Hera, who played a vital role in religious ceremonies, were among the few women allowed to participate in the public rituals of Olympia.

The decline of Olympia began with the Roman conquest of Greece in the 2nd century BCE, though the games continued under Roman rule. The eventual rise of Christianity and the edict of Theodosius I in 393 CE, which banned pagan festivals, marked the end of the ancient games. Earthquakes, floods, and the passage of time further contributed to the site's abandonment and deterioration. It was not until the 19th century, with the rediscovery and excavation of Olympia, that its historical and cultural significance was brought back to light.

Today, Olympia is a place of pilgrimage for history enthusiasts, athletes, and anyone drawn to the ideals of the ancient Greeks. The archaeological site, meticulously preserved and studied, offers a window into a world where sport and spirituality were intertwined. Walking through the ruins, you can almost hear the roar of the crowd, the clash of competitors, and the solemn prayers to the gods. The nearby Archaeological Museum of Olympia houses many of the treasures unearthed at the site, including intricate sculptures, votive offerings, and artifacts that shed light on daily life in ancient Greece.

The modern Olympic Games, revived in 1896, owe their existence to the legacy of Olympia. While the format and scope of the games have evolved, their core values of excellence, friendship, and respect remain rooted in ancient traditions. The lighting of the Olympic flame, the oath of sportsmanship, and the celebration of global unity all trace their origins back to this sacred sanctuary in the Peloponnese.

Olympia represents more than just the birthplace of the Olympic Games; it is a symbol of humanity's enduring quest for greatness. The ideals that once inspired athletes and spectators in this valley continue to resonate across the world, reminding us of the power of sport to unite, inspire, and transcend boundaries. Through its ruins, myths, and traditions, Olympia invites us to reflect on the values that define us and to strive for our own moments of glory.

Delphi: The Oracle and the Center of the Ancient World

Perched on the slopes of Mount Parnassus, overlooking the valley of Phocis, Delphi is one of the most iconic and mystical sites of ancient Greece. Revered as the center of the ancient world, or omphalos, Delphi was a place where gods and mortals intersected, where questions about destiny, politics, and personal trials were answered by the enigmatic Oracle of Apollo. It served not only as a religious sanctuary but also as a cultural and intellectual hub, drawing pilgrims, leaders, and thinkers from across the known world. The influence of Delphi on the spiritual, political, and artistic life of ancient Greece cannot be overstated, and its legacy echoes through history as a symbol of wisdom, mystery, and divine inspiration.

The mythological origins of Delphi are steeped in intrigue and wonder. According to legend, Zeus released two eagles from opposite ends of the earth to find its center. The birds met at Delphi, where the sacred stone known as the omphalos marked the navel of the world. This myth established Delphi as a place of cosmic significance, a link between the heavens and the earth. Another legend tells of Apollo slaying the monstrous serpent Python, which guarded the sanctuary. By defeating Python, Apollo claimed the site as his own, transforming it into a place of prophecy and worship dedicated to the god of music, light, and truth.

Central to Delphi's allure was the Oracle, a priestess known as the Pythia, who served as the mouthpiece of Apollo. Her role was shrouded in ritual and mystery, adding to the sanctity of the site. The Pythia would enter a trance-like state, seated on a tripod above a chasm from which intoxicating vapors were said to rise. In this altered state, she would utter cryptic pronouncements, which were then interpreted by priests and conveyed to those seeking guidance. The questions posed to the Oracle ranged from matters of state—such as whether to go to war or found a colony—to deeply personal dilemmas. Her answers, often ambiguous and open to interpretation, carried immense weight and shaped the decisions of individuals and city-states alike.

The sanctuary of Apollo at Delphi was a sprawling complex of temples, treasuries, monuments, and other structures that reflected the wealth and devotion of the Greek world. At its heart stood the Temple of Apollo, an imposing Doric structure that housed the Oracle. Built and rebuilt multiple times over the centuries due to earthquakes and fires, the temple was adorned with inscriptions, dedications, and statues. One famous inscription on its walls read "Know Thyself," a profound philosophical directive that encapsulated the spirit of Delphi as a place of introspection and enlightenment.

The Sacred Way, a winding path that led through the sanctuary to the Temple of Apollo, was lined with treasuries and votive offerings. These treasuries, built by various city-states, were elaborate structures designed to house gifts to the god. Each treasury was a statement of pride and power, showcasing the wealth and artistic achievements of its patrons. The Treasury of the Athenians, for example, stood out for its intricate carvings and inscriptions, celebrating Athens' victories and contributions to the Panhellenic ideal. The dedication of such treasures also served as a form of diplomacy, reinforcing alliances and rivalries in a highly competitive political landscape.

At the base of the sanctuary, the Castalian Spring provided the sacred water used for purification rituals. Pilgrims, priests, and the Pythia herself would cleanse themselves here before entering the sanctuary. The spring, fed by the pure waters of Mount Parnassus, was considered a source of divine energy, and its connection to Apollo and the Muses further emphasized the spiritual significance of the site. Even today, the tranquil setting of the Castalian Spring exudes an air of timeless serenity.

The theater of Delphi, situated above the Temple of Apollo, was another centerpiece of the sanctuary. With its semicircular rows of stone seats carved into the mountain, the theater could accommodate up to 5,000 spectators. It hosted musical and dramatic performances during the Pythian Games, a Panhellenic festival held every four years in honor of Apollo. These games, second only to the Olympics in prestige, included athletic competitions, chariot races, and artistic contests. The blending of athleticism and artistry reflected the Greek ideal of kalokagathia, the harmony of physical and moral excellence.

Further up the slopes, the stadium of Delphi stands as a testament to the importance of sport in ancient Greek culture. Its long, rectangular track, flanked by stone seats, hosted foot races and other events during the Pythian Games. The stadium's elevated location offered breathtaking views of the sanctuary and the surrounding valley, creating a sense of unity between the natural and the divine. For the athletes who competed here, victory was not only a personal achievement but also a tribute to Apollo and their city-state.

Delphi's influence extended far beyond its physical boundaries. As a Panhellenic sanctuary, it was a place where Greeks from all regions could come together, fostering a sense of shared identity and cultural cohesion. The Oracle's pronouncements shaped the course of history, influencing decisions that ranged from colonization efforts to major political alliances. The Delphic Amphictyony, a council of city-states that managed the sanctuary, served as an early example of cooperative governance, setting a precedent for future forms of political organization.

Art and literature were profoundly influenced by Delphi's legacy. The sanctuary inspired countless works, from the poetry of Pindar, who celebrated the victories of athletes at the Pythian Games, to the tragedies of Aeschylus and Sophocles, which often grappled with themes of prophecy and fate. Sculptors and architects drew inspiration from the sanctuary's monuments, creating masterpieces that reflected the ideals of beauty, harmony, and proportion. The Charioteer of Delphi, a bronze statue discovered at the site, remains one of the finest examples of ancient Greek artistry, capturing the dignity and poise of its subject with exquisite detail.

The decline of Delphi began with the rise of the Roman Empire, though the sanctuary retained its significance for several centuries. The Emperor Hadrian, a great admirer of Greek culture, made substantial contributions to its preservation. However, the spread of Christianity and the edicts of Theodosius I, which banned pagan practices, marked the end of Delphi's religious function. Over time, the site fell into ruin, its treasures looted or lost, and its memory preserved only in the annals of history and the imagination of poets.

The modern rediscovery of Delphi in the 19th century brought its wonders back into the light. Archaeological excavations, spearheaded by French and Greek teams, unearthed the remains of the sanctuary and its artifacts, providing invaluable insights into ancient Greek culture. Today, Delphi is a UNESCO World Heritage Site, attracting visitors from around the world who come to marvel at its ruins and reflect on its enduring legacy. The site's museum houses many of its treasures, including the Charioteer and the omphalos, offering a deeper understanding of its historical and spiritual significance.

Delphi is more than just an archaeological site; it is a place of profound resonance, where the past and present converge. Its myths, rituals, and monuments continue to inspire awe and curiosity, reminding us of the timeless desire to seek knowledge, understand our place in the cosmos, and connect with something greater than ourselves. To walk the Sacred Way, to gaze upon the remnants of the Temple of Apollo, and to stand where the Pythia once prophesied is to touch the essence of a civilization that shaped the foundation of the Western world. Delphi remains, as it was in antiquity, a beacon of wisdom and wonder.

Epidaurus: Theater, Healing, and Ancient Medicine

Tucked into the gentle hills of the northeastern Peloponnese, Epidaurus is a place where art, medicine, and spirituality converged to create one of the most remarkable centers of ancient Greek culture. Revered as a sanctuary of healing and home to one of the most iconic theaters of antiquity, Epidaurus embodies the profound relationship between body, mind, and spirit that defined Greek civilization. This site was not merely a collection of temples and structures; it was a destination for pilgrims seeking cures, a stage for performances that stirred the soul, and a testament to the ingenuity and humanistic values of its creators. Its significance lies not just in its physical remnants but in the enduring ideals it represents.

The star attraction of Epidaurus, and arguably one of the crowning achievements of ancient Greek architecture, is its theater. Built in the 4th century BCE, the Theater of Epidaurus is celebrated for its extraordinary acoustics, elegant design, and harmonious integration with the surrounding landscape. With a capacity of approximately 14,000 spectators, the theater's semi-circular arrangement of limestone seats rises in perfect symmetry, creating an awe-inspiring visual and auditory experience. From the highest row, one can not only hear the softest whisper from the orchestra below but also take in a panoramic view of the lush, rolling hills that embrace the site. This seamless blend of natural and man-made beauty is a hallmark of Greek architectural philosophy, which sought to reflect the balance and order of the cosmos.

The acoustics of the theater have long been a subject of fascination and study. The clarity with which sound travels across its vast expanse is attributed to the carefully calculated design of its tiers and the properties of the limestone used in construction. Modern tests have demonstrated that even a coin dropped in the center of the orchestra can be heard clearly from the uppermost seats. This acoustic perfection allowed for performances of tragedies and comedies to be experienced with equal intensity by all attendees, regardless of their position. The plays performed here, often works by Aeschylus, Sophocles, and Euripides, were not merely entertainment but a form of communal catharsis, exploring themes of morality, fate, and the human condition.

Epidaurus was not solely a place for theatrical performances; it was first and foremost a sanctuary dedicated to Asclepius, the god of medicine and healing. The cult of Asclepius, which flourished here, attracted pilgrims from all corners of the ancient world, seeking relief from ailments both physical and psychological. Central to the sanctuary was the Asklepieion, a complex of buildings that served as a healing center. This sacred precinct included temples, baths, dormitories, and other facilities designed to promote health and well-being. The holistic approach to medicine practiced here combined religious rituals, physical treatments, and psychological support, reflecting a deep understanding of the interconnectedness of body, mind, and spirit.

The Temple of Asclepius, the centerpiece of the sanctuary, was a grand structure adorned with sculptures and inscriptions that celebrated the god's healing powers. Within the temple stood a statue of Asclepius, often depicted holding a staff entwined with a serpent—a symbol that remains associated with medicine to this day. Pilgrims would offer sacrifices and prayers to the god, seeking his favor and intervention. The practice of incubation, or enkoimesis, was a key ritual in the healing process. Patients would spend the night in the abaton, a sacred dormitory, where they believed Asclepius would appear to them in dreams, offering guidance or performing miraculous cures. These dream experiences were then interpreted by priests, who prescribed treatments based on the divine revelations.

The therapeutic practices at Epidaurus were remarkably advanced for their time, blending religious faith with empirical knowledge. The sanctuary's physicians, known as Asclepiads, were trained in various forms of treatment, including dietary regulation, herbal medicine, and surgical procedures. The use of mineral baths, massages, and physical exercise was also common, emphasizing the importance of maintaining a healthy lifestyle. The tholos, a circular building within the sanctuary, is thought to have played a role in these treatments, possibly as a space for purification rituals or consultations. Its intricate design, featuring concentric circles and a labyrinthine arrangement of passages, reflects the sophistication and symbolism that characterized the site.

The Katagogion, a large guesthouse, provided accommodation for the many visitors who flocked to Epidaurus. This structure, with its numerous rooms and courtyards, highlights the scale of operations at the sanctuary and the care taken to ensure the comfort of its guests. Pilgrims often stayed for extended periods, undergoing a combination of medical treatments and spiritual practices. The sense of community fostered by the sanctuary was an integral part of the healing process, as patients drew strength from their shared faith and experiences.

The influence of Epidaurus extended far beyond its immediate surroundings. Its reputation as a center of healing and cultural activity made it a beacon of hope and inspiration throughout the ancient world. The principles of medicine and theater developed here were disseminated across Greece and beyond, shaping the evolution of these disciplines for centuries to come. The sanctuary's emphasis on holistic care and the integration of art and science remain relevant today, offering valuable lessons for modern approaches to health and well-being.

The decline of Epidaurus began with the rise of Christianity, which led to the suppression of pagan cults and the eventual abandonment of the sanctuary. Earthquakes and the passage of time further contributed to the site's deterioration. However, the rediscovery and excavation of Epidaurus in the 19th and 20th centuries brought its wonders back to light, revealing the ingenuity and vision of its creators. Today, the site is a UNESCO World Heritage Site and a popular destination for travelers and scholars alike, drawn by its historical significance and enduring beauty.

Modern performances at the Theater of Epidaurus continue to honor the legacy of its ancient past. Each summer, the Epidaurus Festival brings together actors, directors, and audiences from around the world to experience the power of Greek drama in its original setting. The theater, still acoustically perfect after more than two millennia, serves as a bridge between the ancient and modern worlds, reminding us of the timelessness of art and its ability to connect people across generations.

Epidaurus is more than just a historical site; it is a testament to the ideals and achievements of ancient Greece. Its theater and sanctuary reflect a culture that valued beauty, knowledge, and the pursuit of excellence. The lessons of Epidaurus—its emphasis on holistic care, its celebration of artistic expression, and its commitment to the betterment of humanity—continue to resonate, offering inspiration and guidance for the challenges of the present and the future. To visit Epidaurus is to step into a world where the boundaries between the physical and the spiritual, the scientific and the artistic, dissolve, revealing the profound unity of existence.

Knossos and the Minoan Civilization

Knossos, the legendary seat of the Minoan civilization, lies on the island of Crete, a place that has captivated historians, archaeologists, and travelers for centuries. This ancient city, often referred to as Europe's oldest, is steeped in myth and history, offering a glimpse into a society that flourished between 2000 and 1400 BCE. The Minoans were a sophisticated and enigmatic people, whose advancements in architecture, art, and trade set them apart as one of the most significant early cultures of the Mediterranean. Their legacy, preserved through the ruins of their palaces and the rich tapestry of myths surrounding them, continues to intrigue and inspire.

At the heart of Knossos stands the Palace of Minos, a sprawling complex that serves as a testament to the ingenuity and ambition of the Minoan civilization. Discovered and partially reconstructed by British archaeologist Sir Arthur Evans in the early 20th century, the palace covers an area of approximately 20,000 square meters and features a labyrinthine layout of rooms, corridors, and courtyards. Its design, with its multi-storied buildings, advanced drainage systems, and vibrant frescoes, reflects a level of sophistication that was unparalleled in its time. The palace was not merely a royal residence but a multifunctional center that housed administrative, religious, and economic activities, underscoring the complexity of Minoan society.

The association of Knossos with the myth of the Minotaur has added a layer of mystique to its history. According to Greek mythology, King Minos of Crete commissioned the architect

Daedalus to construct a labyrinth to imprison the Minotaur, a creature born of the union between Minos's wife, Pasiphae, and a divine bull. This labyrinth, often linked to the palace itself due to its intricate design, became the setting for the tale of Theseus, who ventured into its depths to slay the beast and liberate Athens from the burden of tribute. The myth of the Minotaur, while fantastical, reflects the cultural and symbolic significance of Knossos, as well as the enduring fascination with its labyrinthine architecture.

The frescoes of Knossos provide a vivid window into the lives, beliefs, and aesthetics of the Minoans. These wall paintings, executed in vibrant colors and dynamic forms, depict scenes of nature, rituals, and daily activities with a remarkable sense of movement and realism. One of the most famous frescoes, the "Bull-Leaping Fresco," portrays a ceremonial activity in which participants vault over the back of a bull, a practice that may have held religious or symbolic significance. The prominence of bulls in Minoan art and mythology highlights their importance in the culture's iconography, possibly representing strength, fertility, or a connection to the divine.

The Minoans' reverence for nature is evident not only in their art but also in the layout and decoration of their buildings. The Palace of Knossos incorporates open courtyards, light wells, and ventilation shafts, creating a harmonious and airy environment that reflects an intimate relationship with the natural world. The imagery of dolphins, lilies, and other elements of the natural landscape further emphasizes this connection, suggesting a society deeply attuned to its surroundings. This respect for nature, combined with their architectural innovations, speaks to the Minoans' ability to balance functionality with aesthetic beauty.

Religion played a central role in Minoan society, and the Palace of Knossos was likely a focal point for worship. The Minoans practiced a polytheistic faith centered on female deities, often referred to as "Mother Goddesses," who were associated with fertility, agriculture, and the cycles of life. The presence of small shrines, sacred symbols such as the double axe (labrys), and the depiction of priestesses in ritualistic contexts suggest that women held significant roles in both religious and social spheres. The use of sacred spaces, such as the throne room and the central court, for ceremonies and processions further underscores the spiritual dimension of Knossos.

Trade was another cornerstone of Minoan prosperity, and Knossos served as a hub of commerce and cultural exchange. The island of Crete's strategic location in the eastern Mediterranean allowed the Minoans to establish extensive trade networks that connected them with Egypt, the Near East, and other parts of the Aegean world. Evidence of imports such as Egyptian faience, Mesopotamian seals, and precious metals demonstrates the reach and influence of Minoan trade. This interconnectedness not only enriched the material culture of the Minoans but also facilitated the exchange of ideas and technologies, contributing to the vibrancy and diversity of their civilization.

The writing systems developed by the Minoans, known as Linear A and Linear B, provide critical insights into their administrative and economic practices, although much about their language remains a mystery. Linear A, used primarily for religious and ceremonial purposes, has yet to be deciphered, leaving many questions about Minoan beliefs and governance unanswered. Linear B, adapted by the Mycenaeans who succeeded the Minoans, has been deciphered and reveals a bureaucratic system of record-keeping that included inventories, trade records, and resource allocation. These scripts highlight the organizational complexity of Minoan society and their ability to manage a thriving economy.

The decline of the Minoan civilization is a subject of ongoing debate among scholars. While the exact causes remain uncertain, a combination of natural disasters and external pressures likely contributed to their downfall. The eruption of the Thera volcano (modern-day Santorini) around 1600 BCE is often cited as a pivotal event that caused widespread devastation and disrupted trade networks. Subsequent invasions by the Mycenaeans, who established their own presence on Crete, marked the end of Minoan dominance. Despite their decline, the Minoans left an indelible mark on the Aegean world, influencing the art, architecture, and mythology of their successors.

The rediscovery of Knossos by Sir Arthur Evans in 1900 was a watershed moment in the study of ancient civilizations. Evans's excavations and interpretations brought the Minoans to public attention, transforming them from a forgotten people into a celebrated culture. However, his restoration efforts, which included the use of concrete to reconstruct parts of the palace, have sparked controversy among archaeologists and historians. While these interventions have made Knossos more accessible to visitors, they have also raised questions about the authenticity of the site and the extent to which modern perceptions have shaped its presentation.

Today, Knossos is a vibrant archaeological site that attracts visitors from around the world, offering a tangible connection to the Minoan past. Walking through the ruins, one can imagine the bustling activity of the palace, the rituals performed in its sacred spaces, and the artistry of its inhabitants. The nearby Heraklion Archaeological Museum houses many of the artifacts discovered at Knossos, including the iconic Snake Goddess figurines, the Phaistos Disc, and intricately decorated pottery. These objects provide invaluable insights into the daily life, beliefs, and artistic achievements of the Minoans.

Knossos and the Minoan civilization represent a pivotal chapter in the story of human history. Their innovations in architecture, art, and trade laid the foundation for the flourishing of later Greek cultures, while their myths and symbols continue to resonate in the collective imagination. As a place where history and legend intertwine, Knossos invites us to explore the origins of civilization and reflect on the enduring legacy of those who came before us. The Minoans, with their creativity, resilience, and vision, remind us of the boundless potential of human achievement.

Legendary Battles: Thermopylae, Marathon, and Salamis

The battles of Thermopylae, Marathon, and Salamis stand as monumental moments in ancient history, shaping not only the survival of Greece but also the trajectory of Western civilization. These legendary conflicts, fought during the Persian Wars in the 5th century BCE, were clashes of empires, ideologies, and strategies. They showcased the resilience, ingenuity, and unity of the Greek city-states against the seemingly insurmountable might of the Persian Empire. Each battle carried its own unique significance, and together, they forged a narrative of defiance and triumph that resonates across millennia.

Thermopylae, fought in 480 BCE, is perhaps the most iconic of these battles, immortalized in both history and legend. The narrow mountain pass, whose name translates to "The Hot Gates," was the chosen site where a small Greek force, led by King Leonidas of Sparta, would make a heroic stand against the vast Persian army of King Xerxes. The Persian invasion, launched in response to earlier Greek resistance, was a massive undertaking involving an army and navy reportedly numbering in the hundreds of thousands. Xerxes sought not just conquest but retribution, aiming to subjugate the fiercely independent Greek city-states under Persian rule.

The Greek strategy at Thermopylae was brilliantly simple yet daring. By holding the narrow pass, the vastly outnumbered Greek forces could neutralize the tactical advantage of the Persian army's size. Leonidas led a small coalition of Greek city-states, including his 300 elite Spartan warriors, alongside contingents from Thespiae, Thebes, and other allies. The Spartans, renowned for their discipline and martial prowess, were the linchpin of this defense. Over several days of relentless combat, the Greeks held their ground, inflicting heavy losses on the Persian forces. Their superior training and the natural bottleneck of the pass created a deadly trap for the invaders.

The tide turned when a Greek traitor, Ephialtes, revealed a hidden mountain path to the Persians, allowing them to outflank the Greek defenders. Realizing the inevitability of defeat, Leonidas dismissed the bulk of his allies, choosing to remain with his 300 Spartans and a handful of others to fight to the death. Their sacrifice, though a tactical loss, became a rallying cry for Greek resistance. Thermopylae demonstrated the power of courage and unity in the face of overwhelming odds, leaving a legacy that transcends the battlefield. The phrase "Molon Labe," meaning "Come and take them," attributed to Leonidas when asked to surrender his weapons, continues to symbolize defiance and resilience.

While Thermopylae was a heroic stand, the Battle of Marathon in 490 BCE was a decisive Greek victory that set the stage for the events to come. Ten years prior to Thermopylae, the Persian king Darius I sought to punish Athens and Eretria for their support of the Ionian Revolt, a rebellion of Greek city-states in Asia Minor against Persian rule. The Persian forces landed on the plains of Marathon, just 26 miles northeast of Athens, intending to crush Greek resistance and establish a foothold for further invasion.

The Athenian army, led by Miltiades, faced a daunting challenge. Vastly outnumbered, the Athenians relied on their hoplite phalanx, a tightly packed formation of heavily armed infantry, to counter the Persian forces. Miltiades devised a bold and unconventional strategy: he strengthened the flanks of his phalanx while deliberately weakening the center. As the

Persians attacked, the Greek center fell back, drawing the invaders into a trap. The reinforced flanks then closed in, enveloping the Persian army in what became a devastating rout. The Persians fled to their ships, leaving behind thousands of dead.

The victory at Marathon was a turning point for Athens and all of Greece. It demonstrated that the mighty Persian Empire could be defeated and bolstered Greek confidence in their ability to defend their homeland. Moreover, the battle's aftermath inspired the legendary run of the messenger Pheidippides, who is said to have raced from Marathon to Athens to announce the victory before collapsing from exhaustion. Though the historical accuracy of this tale is debated, it gave rise to the modern marathon race, a lasting tribute to the endurance and determination of the Greeks.

The final chapter in this trilogy of legendary battles is the naval engagement at Salamis in 480 BCE. Following the fall of Thermopylae, the Persian army advanced southward, capturing Athens and threatening to overwhelm the Greek resistance. Themistocles, an Athenian general and master strategist, recognized that the key to victory lay in controlling the sea. The Greek navy, though outnumbered, was composed of highly maneuverable triremes, swift warships designed for ramming and close combat. Themistocles lured the Persian fleet into the narrow straits of Salamis, where their numerical advantage would be negated.

The battle unfolded as a masterpiece of naval strategy and deception. Themistocles used a combination of psychological warfare and cunning to bait Xerxes into committing his fleet to the confined waters. Once engaged, the Greek triremes exploited their superior maneuverability, striking the larger Persian ships with precision and ferocity. The straits became a chaotic theater of destruction as Greek and Persian vessels collided, capsized, and sank. Xerxes, watching from a throne on a nearby hill, witnessed the disintegration of his naval power.

The victory at Salamis was a defining moment in the Persian Wars. It shattered the logistical backbone of the Persian invasion, forcing Xerxes to retreat with much of his army. The Greek coalition, now emboldened, would go on to achieve further victories, including the decisive land battle at Plataea in 479 BCE. Salamis not only secured Greek independence but also preserved the cultural and political ideals that would later define Western civilization. The triumph was a testament to the ingenuity and determination of the Greeks, who turned the tide of war through unity and strategic brilliance.

The significance of these battles extends far beyond their immediate outcomes. They were not merely military engagements but existential struggles that determined the fate of Greece and the future of its democratic ideals. The Persian Wars pitted the centralized, autocratic empire of Persia against the decentralized, independent city-states of Greece. The victories at Marathon, Thermopylae, and Salamis ensured the survival of these city-states, allowing their unique political, philosophical, and artistic traditions to flourish. The legacy of these conflicts is evident in the works of Herodotus, Aeschylus, and other chroniclers who immortalized the courage and sacrifice of those who fought.

The lessons of these battles continue to resonate. They remind us of the power of unity in the face of adversity, the importance of strategy and innovation, and the enduring value of personal and collective sacrifice for a greater cause. The Greeks, through their actions and ideals, left a blueprint for resilience and determination that has inspired generations. To walk the fields of Marathon, to stand at the narrow pass of Thermopylae, or to gaze upon the straits of Salamis is to connect with a history that shaped the world as we know it. These legendary battles are not just stories of the past; they are timeless reminders of what can be achieved when courage, strategy, and unity converge.

CHAPTER 5: GREECE'S STUNNING NATURAL LANDSCAPES

Meteora: Monasteries Suspended in the Sky

Rising dramatically from the plains of Thessaly in central Greece, the rock formations of Meteora are a breathtaking testament to nature's artistry and humanity's unyielding faith. Towering sandstone pillars, sculpted over millions of years by wind, water, and geological upheaval, create an otherworldly landscape that feels as though it belongs to a realm beyond earth. Perched precariously atop these natural monoliths are the monasteries of Meteora, remarkable structures that seem to defy gravity and logic. These sacred edifices, built by monks seeking isolation and spiritual connection, create a harmonious blend of human ingenuity and natural wonder. Meteora is not only a stunning visual marvel but also a profound spiritual and historical site that continues to inspire awe in visitors from all corners of the world.

The story of Meteora begins with the formation of its unique rock pillars. Geologists believe that the region was once submerged beneath a prehistoric sea millions of years ago. Over time, sediment deposited at the bottom of this body of water solidified into layers of sandstone and conglomerate. As tectonic forces lifted the land, the sea receded, leaving behind these towering rock formations. Erosion, driven by the relentless power of wind and water, sculpted the rocks into their current shapes, creating sheer cliffs, narrow spires, and rugged peaks. The result is a landscape that feels almost mystical, as though shaped by the hands of gods rather than the forces of nature.

What makes Meteora truly extraordinary, however, is its human history. The name "Meteora" itself means "suspended in the air," a fitting description for the monasteries that crown the summits of these towering pillars. The first monks arrived in Meteora during the 11th century, seeking refuge from political instability and external threats. Drawn by the isolation and the natural fortification offered by the rocks, these hermits lived in caves and crevices, dedicating their lives to prayer and solitude. Over the centuries, this monastic community grew, and by the 14th century, construction began on the monasteries that would make Meteora famous.

Building these monasteries was a feat of engineering and determination. With no roads or modern machinery, the monks had to devise ingenious methods to transport materials to the summits. Ladders, ropes, and nets were used to haul stones, timber, and other supplies up the steep cliffs—a process that could take decades for a single monastery. The isolation of these structures was not merely practical; it was also symbolic. The monks believed that the height and inaccessibility of their monasteries brought them closer to God, creating a physical and spiritual separation from the earthly world below.

At its peak, Meteora was home to 24 monasteries, each a sanctuary of faith, learning, and art. Today, only six of these monasteries remain active, but they continue to function as living centers of Orthodox Christianity. Each monastery has its own unique character and history, reflecting the devotion and creativity of the monks who built and inhabited them. The Great Meteoron Monastery, the largest and oldest of the six, was founded in the 14th century by Saint Athanasios, who is considered the father of the Meteora monastic community. This monastery, with its sprawling complex of chapels, refectories, and libraries, serves as a testament to the enduring legacy of Meteora's spiritual heritage.

Entering one of these monasteries is like stepping back in time. The interiors are adorned with intricate frescoes, icons, and religious artifacts that reflect the Byzantine artistic tradition. These works of art are not merely decorative; they serve as visual representations of theological concepts and narratives, guiding the faithful in their spiritual journey. The frescoes often depict scenes from the Bible, the lives of saints, and the struggles of early Christians, creating a vivid tapestry of faith and devotion. The libraries of Meteora, some of which still hold ancient manuscripts and religious texts, underscore the monasteries' role as centers of learning and preservation.

The natural beauty of Meteora is inseparable from its spiritual significance. The interplay between the rugged rocks and the serene monasteries creates a sense of harmony and balance that resonates deeply with visitors. The awe-inspiring views from the monasteries' balconies, where one can gaze out over the Thessalian plain and the distant Pindus Mountains, evoke a sense of wonder and humility. It is easy to see why the monks believed this place to be sacred, a bridge between heaven and earth.

In addition to its religious and historical importance, Meteora is a haven for outdoor enthusiasts and adventurers. The region offers a variety of activities, from hiking and rock climbing to photography and birdwatching. Trails wind through the landscape, leading visitors to hidden viewpoints, ancient caves, and lesser-known corners of Meteora. For climbers, the vertical cliffs and challenging routes provide an exhilarating experience, combining physical effort with the reward of unparalleled vistas. Even for those who simply wish to wander and explore, the sense of discovery in Meteora is palpable, as each turn reveals new perspectives and hidden treasures.

The preservation of Meteora's natural and cultural heritage is a delicate balance. Recognized as a UNESCO World Heritage Site, the area is protected by strict regulations that aim to safeguard its unique environment and historical significance. Efforts have been made to ensure that tourism does not compromise the spiritual and ecological integrity of the site. Visitors are encouraged to approach Meteora with respect and mindfulness, understanding that it is not only a place of beauty but also a living, breathing community of faith.

Seasonal shifts add another layer of enchantment to Meteora. In spring, wildflowers bloom across the plains, adding bursts of color to the already stunning landscape. Summer brings warm, golden light that bathes the rocks and monasteries in a glow that seems almost ethereal. Autumn transforms the surrounding forests into a tapestry of reds, oranges, and yellows, creating a striking contrast against the gray sandstone. Winter, with its occasional dusting of snow, lends a quiet, contemplative atmosphere to the region, emphasizing its timeless serenity.

Meteora's legacy extends beyond its physical presence. It is a place that invites reflection, offering a sanctuary not only for monks but for anyone seeking solace or inspiration. The monasteries, with their enduring faith and resilience, remind us of the human capacity to create and persevere in the face of seemingly insurmountable challenges. The landscape, shaped by nature's slow and steady hand, serves as a reminder of the passage of time and the interconnectedness of all things.

For those who visit Meteora, the experience is unforgettable. The combination of natural grandeur, historical depth, and spiritual resonance creates a sense of connection that lingers long after one has left. To stand among the towering rocks, to walk the paths once trodden by monks, and to gaze upon the monasteries suspended in the sky is to witness a place where the boundaries between the earthly and the divine blur, leaving a lasting impression on the soul.

Mount Olympus: Home of the Gods

Rising majestically from the Thermaic Gulf in northern Greece, Mount Olympus is not just a mountain but a symbol of divinity, history, and natural splendor. Its sheer peaks, shrouded in mist and mystery, have captured the imagination of countless generations. To the ancient Greeks, this was no ordinary mountain; it was the sacred dwelling of the Olympian gods, a place where mortals dared not tread without reverence. Today, Mount Olympus stands as a UNESCO Biosphere Reserve, celebrated for its unique biodiversity and its cultural significance. This blend of mythology and natural beauty makes it one of Greece's most captivating landmarks, drawing pilgrims, hikers, and adventurers alike to its towering heights.

The mythology of Mount Olympus is as towering as the mountain itself. In Greek mythology, Olympus was believed to be the home of the twelve Olympian gods, led by Zeus, the king of the gods. Perched high above the mortal world, the gods were said to reside in an opulent palace atop the mountain's summit, surrounded by clouds that shielded them from human eyes. The myths paint this as a place of eternal feasting, divine deliberations, and unimaginable splendor. Each god had their domain within Olympus—Zeus ruled with his thunderbolts, Hera presided over marriage and family, and Athena brought wisdom and strategy. It was a realm of power, beauty, and the source of countless stories that have endured through the ages.

The peaks of Mount Olympus are named in homage to its mythological past. Mytikas, the highest peak at 2,917 meters, is said to have been the throne of Zeus himself, where he surveyed the world below and dispensed his judgments. Stefani, another prominent peak, is often referred to as the "Throne of Zeus" due to its dramatic, crown-like appearance. These peaks were not merely geographical features to the ancient Greeks but sacred places imbued with the presence of the divine. Even the lower slopes of the mountain were considered hallowed ground, with shrines and altars dedicated to the gods scattered throughout the region.

The human connection to Mount Olympus is not confined to mythology. Archaeological evidence suggests that the area around the mountain has been inhabited since the Neolithic period, and its slopes were home to ancient sanctuaries and settlements. The city of Dion, located at the base of Mount Olympus, was a significant religious center in antiquity. Dedicated to Zeus, Dion was a place where festivals, sacrifices, and athletic competitions were held in honor of the gods. Excavations at Dion have uncovered temples, theaters, and mosaics that offer a glimpse into the spiritual and cultural life of those who lived in the shadow of the mountain.

For modern visitors, Mount Olympus offers a different kind of pilgrimage—one that celebrates its natural beauty and the sense of adventure it inspires. The mountain is a paradise for hikers and climbers, with well-marked trails that lead through forests, gorges, and alpine meadows to its towering peaks. The E4 European long-distance path, which traverses Greece, passes through Mount Olympus, making it accessible to both seasoned mountaineers and casual trekkers. Each trail offers its own unique experience, from the lush woodlands of the lower slopes to the stark, rocky landscapes near the summit. Along the way, visitors encounter breathtaking vistas, cascading waterfalls, and an ever-changing tapestry of flora and fauna.

Mount Olympus is home to a remarkable range of ecosystems, thanks to its varied altitude and climate. The lower slopes are dominated by dense forests of oak, beech, and pine, providing shelter for wildlife such as deer, foxes, and wild boar. Higher up, the vegetation thins out, giving way to alpine meadows adorned with rare wildflowers and herbs. These high-altitude zones are inhabited by hardy species like chamois and golden eagles, which thrive in the rugged terrain. The mountain's biodiversity is further enriched by its endemic species—plants and animals found nowhere else in the world. This ecological richness has earned Mount Olympus its designation as a UNESCO Biosphere Reserve, underscoring its importance as a natural treasure.

One of the most striking features of Mount Olympus is the Enipeas Gorge, a dramatic canyon carved by the Enipeas River. This gorge, with its steep cliffs, crystal-clear streams, and lush vegetation, is a favorite destination for hikers and nature lovers. The trail through the gorge, part of the ascent to the mountain's peaks, offers a journey through a landscape that seems untouched by time. Wooden bridges cross the river at several points, and the sound of cascading waterfalls accompanies travelers as they make their way through this enchanting terrain. The gorge is also home to caves and rock formations that have inspired local legends, adding another layer of mystique to the mountain.

Reaching the summit of Mount Olympus is a challenge that rewards both body and spirit. The most popular route begins at Prionia, a mountain refuge located at an elevation of 1,100 meters. From there, the trail ascends through dense forests and rocky terrain, eventually leading to the Spilios Agapitos Refuge, a mountain hut where climbers can rest and acclimate before making their final push to the summit. The ascent to Mytikas, the highest peak, is a demanding climb that requires careful navigation and a good level of fitness. For those who reach the summit, the sense of achievement is matched only by the awe-inspiring views that stretch across the Aegean Sea and the distant landscapes of Macedonia and Thessaly.

The spiritual resonance of Mount Olympus is not lost on those who visit. Whether or not one believes in the ancient myths, there is something undeniably transcendent about standing on the slopes of a mountain that has been revered for millennia. The sheer scale of Olympus, combined with its natural beauty and historical significance, creates an experience that is both humbling and uplifting. Many visitors describe a sense of connection to something greater than themselves, as if the mountain's enduring presence offers a glimpse into the eternal.

Seasonal changes only enhance the allure of Mount Olympus. In spring, the lower slopes come alive with blooming wildflowers and the fresh green of new growth. Summer offers the best conditions for climbing, with clear skies and warm temperatures that make the trails more accessible. Autumn brings a riot of color to the forests, as the leaves turn shades of red, orange, and gold. Winter, though more challenging, transforms the mountain into a snow-covered wonderland, attracting experienced climbers and adventurers who relish the solitude and stark beauty of the season.

Efforts to preserve Mount Olympus and its cultural heritage are ongoing. The mountain is protected as part of the Olympus National Park, established in 1938 as Greece's first national park. This designation reflects a commitment to safeguarding its unique ecosystems and historical sites for future generations. Sustainable tourism initiatives aim to balance the needs of visitors with the importance of conservation, ensuring that the mountain remains a source of inspiration and wonder for years to come.

Mount Olympus is more than just a geographical landmark; it is a symbol of human aspiration, resilience, and reverence for the natural world. To stand in its shadow, to walk its trails, or to gaze upon its peaks is to step into a story that stretches across centuries—a story of gods and mortals, of nature and mythology, of challenges and triumphs. Whether viewed from afar or experienced up close, Mount Olympus continues to captivate all who encounter it, offering a reminder of the enduring power of both nature and imagination.

Vikos Gorge: Europe's Deepest Canyon

Carved into the rugged terrain of northern Greece, the Vikos Gorge is one of the most striking natural wonders in Europe. Nestled within the Pindus Mountains and forming the heart of the Vikos–Aoös National Park, this geological marvel holds the distinction of being among the deepest gorges in the world relative to its width. Its dramatic cliffs, plunging as deep as 1,000 meters in some sections, are a testament to millions of years of erosion, while the lush vegetation and crystal-clear waters below create an ecosystem teeming with life. For those who venture into its depths or stand on its precipices, Vikos Gorge offers not only awe-inspiring views but also a sense of connection to a landscape that has remained largely untouched by time.

The formation of Vikos Gorge is a story written in stone, shaped by the relentless forces of water and time. Over millennia, the Voidomatis River, a tributary of the Aoös River, carved its way through the limestone and dolomite rock, creating the gorge's steep walls and intricate contours. The geological composition of the area, a mix of sedimentary and metamorphic rock layers, adds to its visual and scientific intrigue. Fossilized remains of marine life found within the rock strata are reminders of a distant past when the region was submerged under an ancient sea. Today, the gorge stands as a natural monument, its towering cliffs and narrow floor offering a stark yet beautiful contrast.

Exploring the Vikos Gorge is an adventure that rewards perseverance and curiosity. The most popular way to experience its grandeur is by hiking the trail that traverses the gorge from the village of Monodendri to Vikos. This 12-kilometer trek is not for the faint of heart, as it requires navigating uneven terrain, steep descents, and occasional river crossings. Yet, for those who embrace the challenge, the journey is unforgettable. Along the way, hikers encounter a landscape of dramatic contrasts: dense forests of oak, pine, and beech that give way to open stretches of rocky terrain; quiet glades where the light filters softly through the trees; and panoramic viewpoints that offer breathtaking vistas of the gorge's sheer cliffs.

One of the highlights of the hike is the Voidomatis River, whose crystal-clear waters meander through the gorge. Fed by natural springs, the river is among the cleanest in Europe, its turquoise hue a striking feature of the landscape. In the summer months, the river becomes a refreshing oasis for hikers, offering a chance to cool off and marvel at the pristine environment. The Voidomatis is also a vital lifeline for the region's flora and fauna, supporting a diverse range of species that thrive in the gorge's unique microclimate.

The biodiversity of Vikos Gorge is nothing short of extraordinary. Its steep cliffs, shaded ravines, and sheltered riverbanks create a variety of habitats that support a wide array of plant and animal life. The gorge is home to over 1,700 species of plants, including several rare and endemic varieties. Among these are medicinal herbs such as oregano, sage, and St. John's wort, which have been used in traditional remedies for centuries. The region's fauna is equally diverse, with species ranging from golden eagles and griffon vultures that soar above the cliffs to brown bears and wolves that roam the surrounding forests. This rich biodiversity has earned Vikos Gorge its status as a protected area within the Vikos–Aoös National Park.

The cultural heritage of the region is as compelling as its natural beauty. The villages that dot the area around the gorge, collectively known as the Zagori villages, are renowned for their traditional stone architecture and timeless charm. These settlements, such as Monodendri, Papingo, and Vikos, serve as gateways to the gorge, offering a glimpse into a way of life that has endured for generations. The stone bridges that span the Voidomatis River, with their graceful arches and sturdy construction, are masterpieces of craftsmanship, reflecting the ingenuity and resilience of the local communities. Many of these bridges date back to the Ottoman period and continue to stand as enduring symbols of the region's history.

Standing at the Oxya viewpoint near Monodendri, one can truly appreciate the scale and majesty of Vikos Gorge. From this vantage point, the gorge unfolds like a natural amphitheater, its walls rising dramatically on either side and converging in the distance. The sense of scale is almost overwhelming, as one contemplates the sheer verticality of the cliffs and the narrow strip of greenery far below. The Oxya viewpoint, along with the neighboring Beloi viewpoint, provides some of the best panoramas of the gorge, making them must-visit spots for photographers and nature enthusiasts.

Seasonal changes bring new dimensions to the Vikos Gorge experience. In spring, the slopes burst into life with wildflowers and blossoming trees, while the river swells with snowmelt, creating a dynamic and vibrant landscape. Summer offers clear skies and warm temperatures, ideal for hiking and exploring. Autumn transforms the gorge into a tapestry of red, orange, and gold, as the forests don their fall colors. Winter, though more challenging for visitors, cloaks the gorge in a serene stillness, with snow-capped peaks and frost-laden trees adding a touch of magic to the scene. Each season offers its own unique perspective, ensuring that no two visits are ever the same.

The preservation of Vikos Gorge is a testament to the importance of sustainable tourism and conservation efforts. The establishment of the Vikos–Aoös National Park in 1973 marked a crucial step in protecting the gorge and its surrounding ecosystems. Today, the park is managed with a focus on maintaining its ecological integrity while allowing visitors to appreciate its beauty responsibly. Local initiatives, such as guided eco-tours and educational programs, aim to raise awareness about the importance of preserving this natural treasure for future generations.

For those who visit Vikos Gorge, the experience is transformative. The sheer scale and raw beauty of the landscape inspire a sense of wonder and humility, reminding us of the power and resilience of nature. Walking its trails, hearing the rush of the Voidomatis River, and gazing up at the towering cliffs evoke a sense of connection to a world that is both ancient and timeless. Vikos Gorge is not just a place to see; it is a place to feel, to reflect, and to be reminded of the profound beauty that exists in the natural world.

The Blue Caves of Zakynthos

The Blue Caves of Zakynthos are a true masterpiece of nature, a series of sea-carved wonders that shimmer with an almost otherworldly beauty. Located along the northern coast of the Greek island of Zakynthos (also known as Zante), these caves are famed for their mesmerizing interplay of light and water, which creates a kaleidoscope of dazzling blue hues. The caves, shaped by centuries of erosion, are both a geological marvel and a haven for marine life. Their allure lies not only in their striking appearance but also in the sense of mystery and tranquility they evoke, making them a must-visit destination for travelers seeking the extraordinary.

Discovered in 1897, the Blue Caves have entranced visitors with their natural charm ever since. Accessible only by sea, these formations are scattered along the rugged coastline between Cape Skinari and Agios Nikolaos. The caves are characterized by their arch-like entrances, eroded into the limestone cliffs by the relentless motion of waves. These arches, some large enough to accommodate small boats, lead into chambers that open up to reveal shimmering pools of azure. The refracted sunlight, combined with the clarity of the Ionian Sea, produces an effect where the water and walls seem to glow with an almost neon intensity. This visual phenomenon is what gives the Blue Caves their name and their enduring allure.

One of the most striking features of the Blue Caves is the way light behaves within them. The sunlight penetrates the water, bouncing off the white limestone seabed and illuminating the caves from below. This creates a surreal effect where the water appears to glow in shades of electric blue, aquamarine, and turquoise. The colors shift and dance with the movement of the waves, making each moment unique. Visitors often find themselves transfixed by the ethereal beauty of this natural light show, a reminder of the interplay between the elements that has shaped this coastline over millennia.

The journey to the Blue Caves is an adventure in itself. Most visitors reach the caves by boat, departing from nearby ports such as Agios Nikolaos or the more distant Zakynthos Town. The trip along the coast offers stunning views of the island's cliffs, hidden coves, and the endless expanse of the Ionian Sea. As the boat approaches the caves, the anticipation builds as the first glimmers of blue come into view. Smaller boats or inflatable dinghies are often used to navigate the tighter channels and arches, allowing visitors to fully immerse themselves in the experience. For the more adventurous, kayaking or paddleboarding offers an intimate and eco-friendly way to explore these natural wonders.

Swimming inside the Blue Caves is an unforgettable experience. The water, crystalline and inviting, is at its most vibrant when viewed from within the caves. Many visitors choose to dive into the water, finding themselves surrounded by a luminous blue that seems almost unreal. The sensation of swimming in what feels like liquid light is both exhilarating and calming, a moment of connection with the natural world that lingers long after leaving. For snorkelers and divers, the caves reveal even more of their secrets beneath the surface, with underwater arches, tunnels, and a variety of marine life awaiting discovery.

The marine ecosystem of the Blue Caves is as captivating as the caves themselves. The pristine waters are home to a diverse array of sea creatures, from schools of shimmering fish to the occasional loggerhead sea turtle (Caretta caretta), a species that Zakynthos is famous for protecting. The caves provide shelter and breeding grounds for various species, making them a vital part of the local marine environment. The clarity of the water allows snorkelers and divers to observe this underwater world in remarkable detail, adding another layer of wonder to the experience.

The geology of the Blue Caves reveals the slow, patient work of nature over countless years. The caves are part of the island's karst landscape, formed by the dissolution of soluble rocks such as limestone. The constant action of waves against the cliffs, combined with the chemical processes of erosion, has sculpted these intricate formations. The arches, chambers, and tunnels that define the caves are a testament to the power of water to shape the earth, creating structures that are as fragile as they are enduring. The ongoing interaction between rock and sea ensures that the Blue Caves are constantly changing, albeit at a pace imperceptible to the human eye.

Photography enthusiasts find the Blue Caves to be a dream destination. The interplay of light, water, and rock creates endless opportunities for capturing stunning images. From the reflections on the water's surface to the glowing walls of the caves, every angle offers a new perspective. Early morning or late afternoon visits are particularly rewarding, as the low angle of the sun enhances the intensity of the colors. However, the challenge lies in capturing the true essence of the caves, as no photograph can fully convey the immersive experience of being there.

The Blue Caves are not only a natural treasure but also a symbol of the island's rich cultural and historical heritage. Zakynthos has long been celebrated for its beauty, inspiring poets, artists, and travelers throughout history. The island's Venetian influence, evident in its architecture and traditions, adds a layer of cultural depth to the experience of visiting the caves. For the locals, the Blue Caves are a source of pride, a reminder of the island's unique identity and its connection to the sea.

Preserving the Blue Caves is a responsibility that falls to both locals and visitors. The fragile ecosystem and geological features of the caves require careful management to ensure their longevity. Sustainable tourism practices, such as limiting the size and number of boats allowed to enter the caves, are essential to minimizing environmental impact. Visitors are encouraged to respect the natural environment, refraining from littering or disturbing the marine life that calls the caves home. By treading lightly, future generations can continue to enjoy the beauty and wonder of this extraordinary place.

The Blue Caves are a testament to the power of nature to inspire and uplift. They are a place where the boundaries between land and sea blur, creating a world that feels both ancient and timeless. Whether it's the thrill of exploring their hidden chambers, the serenity of floating in their glowing waters, or the joy of simply gazing at their beauty, the Blue Caves leave an indelible mark on all who visit. They are a reminder of the treasures that lie beneath the surface, waiting to be discovered by those who seek them with an open heart and a sense of wonder.

Samaria Gorge: Crete's Hiking Haven

Samaria Gorge, nestled within the rugged White Mountains of Crete, is a natural masterpiece carved by time and shaped by the elements. Spanning 16 kilometers in length, it holds the title of Europe's longest gorge and is undoubtedly one of Greece's most renowned hiking destinations. Known for its dramatic landscapes, rich biodiversity, and historical significance, Samaria Gorge offers an unforgettable experience for those who venture into its depths. It is not just a hike; it is a journey through a landscape that feels untouched by time, where every step reveals new marvels and every turn tells a story. The gorge is a place where nature, history, and adventure converge, creating an unmatched sense of wonder for all who visit.

Samaria Gorge begins at Xyloskalo, a steep and narrow descent situated at an altitude of 1,230 meters on the Omalos Plateau. The name "Xyloskalo," which translates to "wooden staircase," refers to the wooden steps that once marked the start of the trail. Today, this entry point has been modernized, but it retains its reputation as a gateway to one of Crete's most challenging and rewarding hikes. The trail winds its way downward, immediately immersing hikers in the breathtaking scenery of the gorge. Towering cliffs rise on either side, their jagged edges outlined against the clear blue sky, while a canopy of pine and cypress offers welcome shade during the initial descent.

The first section of the hike is marked by the scent of pine needles crushed underfoot and the occasional sound of rushing water from hidden springs. As you descend deeper, the towering walls of the gorge begin to close in, creating a sense of being enveloped by the raw power of nature. The trail is well-maintained but uneven, with loose stones and rocky patches that demand careful footing. For many hikers, this part of the journey is a test of endurance, as the steep decline can be tough on the legs. However, the effort is rewarded by the unfolding beauty of the gorge, which reveals itself layer by layer like a carefully unwrapped gift.

About halfway through the hike lies the abandoned village of Samaria, a poignant reminder of the human history intertwined with this natural wonder. Once home to shepherds and villagers who lived off the land, the settlement was abandoned in the 1960s when the area was declared a national park. Today, the stone houses stand as silent witnesses to a way of life that has all but disappeared. The village offers a tranquil spot for rest and reflection, with benches shaded by ancient trees and the soft murmur of the Tarraios River nearby. It is here that many hikers pause to catch their breath and absorb the unique atmosphere of this remote and hauntingly beautiful location.

The flora and fauna of Samaria Gorge are as diverse as its landscapes. The gorge is home to over 450 species of plants, many of which are endemic to Crete and protected by law. Among the most iconic of these is the Cretan maple, which thrives in the rocky terrain, and the rare dittany, a herb prized since ancient times for its medicinal properties. The gorge is also a sanctuary for wildlife, including the elusive kri-kri, or Cretan wild goat, which roams the cliffs with an agility that seems almost supernatural. Birds of prey, such as griffon vultures and golden eagles, can often be seen circling overhead, their cries echoing through the canyon. This rich biodiversity is part of what makes Samaria Gorge a UNESCO Biosphere Reserve, a designation that underscores its ecological importance.

As the hike progresses, the gorge narrows dramatically, culminating in its most famous feature: the Iron Gates. Here, the towering walls of the gorge stand just three meters apart, creating a natural corridor that is both awe-inspiring and humbling. Walking through the Iron Gates feels like stepping into another world, one where the forces of nature reign supreme. The sunlight filters through the narrow opening, casting shifting patterns of light and shadow on the rocky walls. It is a moment of pure immersion in the grandeur of the natural world, a highlight of the journey that leaves a lasting impression on all who pass through.

Beyond the Iron Gates, the trail begins to level out, signaling the final stretch of the hike. The landscape opens up, offering a glimpse of the Libyan Sea in the distance. The path follows the course of the Tarraios River, which flows gently toward the village of Agia Roumeli, the endpoint of the trek. This small coastal village, accessible only by foot or boat, is a haven for weary hikers. Here, the whitewashed buildings and tranquil beaches provide a stark contrast to the rugged terrain of the gorge. Many visitors take a moment to rest and refresh themselves with a swim in the crystal-clear waters of the sea, a fitting end to the journey.

Hiking Samaria Gorge is not just a physical challenge but also a cultural and historical experience. The gorge has been a passageway for centuries, used by shepherds, merchants, and even resistance fighters during times of conflict. During World War II, the gorge served as a refuge for Cretan partisans and Allied soldiers, who used its hidden paths and caves to evade capture. This history adds a layer of depth to the hike, as every step takes you through a landscape that has witnessed both the triumphs and struggles of those who came before.

The best time to visit Samaria Gorge is during the spring and autumn months when the weather is mild, and the trail is at its most inviting. Spring brings a burst of color to the gorge, as wildflowers bloom and the rivers flow with melted snow from the mountains. Autumn, with its cooler temperatures and golden hues, offers a quieter and more contemplative experience. The gorge is closed during the winter months due to the risk of flash floods and unstable terrain, a reminder of the raw power of nature that defines this remarkable place.

Preserving the natural beauty and ecological integrity of Samaria Gorge is a priority for local authorities and conservationists. The designation of the area as a national park in 1962 was a landmark decision that has helped protect its unique environment. Efforts are ongoing to manage tourism sustainably, ensuring that the thousands of visitors who hike the gorge each year do not harm its delicate ecosystems. Hikers are encouraged to follow the Leave No Trace principles, taking care to carry out all waste and avoid disturbing the wildlife. These measures are essential to maintaining the pristine condition of the gorge for future generations.

For those who tackle the hike, Samaria Gorge is more than just a destination; it is a journey of discovery and transformation. The physical effort required to traverse its rugged terrain is matched by the emotional and spiritual rewards of immersing oneself in such a stunning and untamed landscape. The gorge challenges and inspires in equal measure, offering a reminder of the beauty and resilience of the natural world. Whether you are drawn by the thrill of adventure, the call of the wild, or the chance to connect with history and culture, Samaria Gorge promises an experience that will stay with you long after you leave its rocky embrace.

Lake Plastira: A Hidden Gem in Central Greece

Nestled in the heart of central Greece, Lake Plastira is a serene sanctuary that combines natural beauty, human ingenuity, and tranquility in one breathtaking setting. Often referred to as the "Little Switzerland" of Greece, this artificial lake is surrounded by dense forests, rolling hills, and the majestic peaks of the Agrafa Mountains. Its pristine waters and unspoiled environment make it a hidden gem, far removed from the bustling tourist hotspots of the Aegean Islands or the classical ruins of Athens. For those who seek peace, outdoor adventure, or a deeper connection to nature, Lake Plastira offers a uniquely rewarding experience that feels both intimate and invigorating.

Lake Plastira owes its existence to a visionary idea born in the mid-20th century. General Nikolaos Plastiras, for whom the lake is named, conceived the plan to harness the region's water resources for irrigation and electricity generation. The Tavropos River, which once flowed freely through the Agrafa region, was dammed in the 1950s, resulting in the creation of the lake. What began as a practical solution to water management soon evolved into something far more significant. The reservoir transformed the surrounding landscape, creating a harmonious balance between human intervention and natural beauty. Today, Lake Plastira is not only a key source of water and energy but also a beloved destination for locals and travelers alike.

The lake's setting is nothing short of idyllic. Surrounded by lush forests of oak, chestnut, and fir, the area exudes a sense of calm and seclusion. The serene waters, which mirror the surrounding mountains and skies, create a picture-perfect vista that changes character with the seasons. In spring, wildflowers carpet the hillsides, adding bursts of color to the landscape. Summer brings long, sunlit days that highlight the lake's turquoise hues. Autumn transforms the forests into a kaleidoscope of reds, oranges, and yellows, while winter blankets the region in snow, lending a quiet, magical atmosphere to the lake's shores.

Exploring Lake Plastira is a journey that can be tailored to every traveler's pace and preference. For those who enjoy outdoor activities, the lake offers a wealth of opportunities to engage with the surrounding environment. Canoeing and kayaking are particularly popular, allowing visitors to glide across the calm waters and take in the scenery from a unique vantage point. The lake's gentle currents and well-marked areas make it suitable for both beginners and experienced paddlers. Fishing enthusiasts will find the lake teeming with species such as trout, carp, and perch, making it an ideal spot for casting a line and enjoying the serenity of nature.

Hiking trails around Lake Plastira provide another way to immerse oneself in its beauty. Trails of varying difficulty wind through the surrounding forests, leading to hidden viewpoints, cascading streams, and charming villages. One particularly rewarding route takes hikers to the Koroni Monastery, perched on a rocky outcrop overlooking the lake. This 12th-century monastery, dedicated to the Virgin Mary, is a place of quiet reflection and offers sweeping views of the lake and the surrounding mountains. The journey to the monastery is as captivating as the destination itself, with the trail passing through shaded woods and open meadows that reveal the region's diverse flora and fauna.

The villages that dot the shores of Lake Plastira are an integral part of its charm. Each village has its own character, from the traditional stone houses of Kastania to the lively tavernas and shops of Neochori. These settlements offer a glimpse into rural Greek life, where hospitality and tradition remain central to daily life. Visitors can enjoy hearty local cuisine, such as slow-cooked lamb, wild mushrooms, and handmade pies, often accompanied by a glass of tsipouro or locally produced wine. The warmth of the villagers and the authenticity of their way of life add depth to the Lake Plastira experience, creating memories that linger long after the trip is over.

Cycling enthusiasts will find Lake Plastira a paradise for exploration on two wheels. The area features a network of cycling routes that cater to all skill levels, from leisurely rides along the lake's perimeter to challenging ascents through the nearby mountains. The well-maintained paths provide a safe and enjoyable way to explore the region, with opportunities to stop and admire the scenery along the way. Renting a bike is easy, with several local businesses offering equipment and advice for those eager to embark on their cycling adventure.

The biodiversity of the Lake Plastira region is a treasure trove for nature lovers. The lake and its surrounding wetlands are home to a variety of bird species, including herons, kingfishers, and kestrels, making it a popular destination for birdwatching. The forests and meadows, meanwhile, support a range of wildlife, from deer and foxes to rare butterflies and amphibians. Conservation efforts have ensured that this delicate ecosystem remains intact, allowing visitors to enjoy its wonders while preserving it for future generations. The balance between human activity and natural preservation is a hallmark of Lake Plastira's appeal.

For those who seek relaxation and rejuvenation, Lake Plastira's tranquil atmosphere provides the perfect escape. The gentle sounds of water lapping against the shore, the rustling of leaves in the breeze, and the distant calls of birds create a symphony of nature that soothes the soul. Several lakeside accommodations, ranging from cozy guesthouses to boutique hotels, offer comfortable retreats where visitors can unwind and take in the views. Many of these establishments emphasize sustainability, incorporating eco-friendly practices and showcasing the region's natural materials and aesthetics.

Cultural events and festivals around Lake Plastira add a lively dimension to the experience. Seasonal celebrations, such as the Feast of the Virgin Mary or the annual Mushroom Festival, bring the community together and offer visitors a chance to participate in local traditions. These events often feature music, dance, and culinary delights, providing a window into the cultural heritage of the region. The blend of natural beauty and cultural vibrancy makes Lake Plastira a destination that appeals to both the heart and the mind.

The changing seasons bring new opportunities to enjoy Lake Plastira's offerings. Winter, in particular, transforms the lake into a snowy wonderland, with opportunities for skiing and snowshoeing in the nearby mountains. The crisp air and serene landscape create an atmosphere of quiet contemplation, making it an ideal time for those who wish to escape the crowds and reconnect with nature. The lake's frozen edges and frosted trees add a touch of enchantment, creating scenes that seem plucked from a fairytale.

Preserving the natural and cultural heritage of Lake Plastira is a shared responsibility. Local authorities and communities have implemented measures to ensure that tourism remains sustainable and respectful of the environment. Visitors are encouraged to minimize their impact by adhering to principles such as reducing waste, respecting wildlife, and supporting local businesses. These efforts not only protect the lake's ecosystem but also enhance the experience for those who come to appreciate its beauty.

Lake Plastira is more than just a destination; it is a journey into the heart of Greece's natural and cultural richness. Its tranquil waters, verdant surroundings, and welcoming communities create a sense of harmony that resonates with all who visit. Whether you come for adventure, relaxation, or simply to marvel at its beauty, Lake Plastira promises an experience that is as enriching as it is unforgettable. It is a place where time slows down, where nature and humanity coexist in perfect balance, and where every moment feels like a gift.

CHAPTER 6: GREEK CUISINE – A FEAST FOR THE SENSES

An Introduction to Greek Food Culture

Greek food culture is a vibrant tapestry woven from centuries of history, geography, and tradition. It is not merely a way of eating but a way of life, deeply rooted in the Mediterranean's bountiful resources and the shared moments of community that food fosters. From the bustling streets of Athens to the quiet villages tucked into mountain valleys, the culinary traditions of Greece reveal a profound respect for the land, the sea, and the seasons. Every meal tells a story—not just of ingredients and preparation but of the people who have preserved these recipes through time, adapting them to changing circumstances while remaining true to their essence. Greek food culture is as much about connection as it is about flavor, making it a cornerstone of the country's identity.

The foundation of Greek cuisine lies in its use of simple, high-quality ingredients. Olive oil, often referred to as "liquid gold," forms the backbone of nearly every dish. Pressed from olives grown in the rocky groves that stretch across the mainland and islands, this oil is more than a cooking medium—it is a symbol of Greek life, health, and prosperity. Vegetables, particularly tomatoes, eggplants, zucchini, and peppers, are celebrated for their freshness and versatility. Herbs like oregano, thyme, and rosemary, often plucked wild from the hillsides, lend their aromatic depth to countless recipes. Cheese, especially feta, is ubiquitous, crumbled over salads or baked into savory pies. The emphasis on unprocessed, seasonal ingredients is not a recent trend but a philosophy handed down through generations.

Seafood occupies a prominent place in Greek food culture, particularly in coastal regions and on the islands. The Aegean and Ionian Seas provide a rich bounty of fish and shellfish, which are prepared with minimal fuss to let their natural flavors shine. Grilled octopus, drizzled with olive oil and lemon, is a beloved delicacy, while sardines and anchovies are often enjoyed marinated or baked. Larger fish like sea bream and red mullet are typically grilled whole, accompanied by nothing more than a squeeze of citrus and a sprinkle of herbs. The freshness of the catch is paramount, and it's not uncommon for diners to select their fish directly from the day's haul at a seaside taverna.

Meat dishes hold a special place in Greek cuisine, often reserved for family gatherings, celebrations, or religious festivals. Lamb and goat, favored for their flavor and cultural significance, are prepared in a myriad of ways—from slow-roasting on a spit during Easter to being stewed with vegetables in hearty casseroles. Pork, chicken, and beef also feature prominently, with dishes like souvlaki, skewered and grilled to perfection, becoming a global ambassador of Greek street food. Moussaka, a baked dish of layered eggplant, minced meat, and béchamel sauce, is another classic that showcases the country's ability to combine bold flavors with comforting textures.

Bread is the cornerstone of every Greek table, symbolizing sustenance and hospitality. Whether it's a rustic village loaf baked in a wood-fired oven or the sesame-studded koulouri sold by street vendors, bread is ever-present. It is used to scoop up dips like tzatziki, a blend of yogurt, cucumber, and garlic, or melitzanosalata, a smoky eggplant spread. Paximadi, a twice-baked barley rusk, is a Cretan specialty often soaked in olive oil and topped with tomatoes and cheese for a simple yet satisfying meal. Bread is more than just food—it is a communal thread that ties diners together, embodying the Greek ethos of sharing.

No discussion of Greek food culture would be complete without mentioning meze, the small dishes served as appetizers or as a meal in their own right. Meze is not just about the food but the act of gathering and sharing, a ritual that fosters connection and conversation. Plates of dolmades, vine leaves stuffed with rice and herbs, sit alongside bowls of taramasalata, a creamy fish roe dip. Saganaki, fried cheese served sizzling in its pan, is a crowd-pleaser, while keftedes, spiced meatballs, offer a burst of flavor in every bite. Meze is often accompanied by ouzo or tsipouro, traditional spirits that add to the convivial atmosphere.

Greek food culture is inseparable from its religious and seasonal rhythms. Orthodox Christianity plays a significant role in shaping culinary practices, particularly during periods of fasting. Lent, for instance, calls for abstaining from meat, dairy, and fish, leading to the creation of delicious plant-based dishes that highlight legumes, grains, and vegetables. Easter, on the other hand, is a time of indulgence, marked by the roasting of lamb and the baking of tsoureki, a sweet, braided bread. Seasonal festivals, such as the grape harvest in autumn or the olive harvest in winter, further underscore the connection between food, faith, and the cycles of nature.

Desserts in Greek cuisine are a celebration of sweetness and tradition. Honey, a staple ingredient revered since antiquity, features prominently in treats like baklava, layers of phyllo dough filled with nuts and soaked in syrup. Loukoumades, deep-fried dough balls drizzled with honey and sprinkled with cinnamon, are a favorite at festivals and family gatherings. Galaktoboureko, a custard-filled pastry, and kourabiedes, almond cookies dusted with powdered sugar, are often prepared for special occasions. These desserts, rich yet not overly complex, reflect the Greek penchant for balancing sweetness with subtlety.

Beverages are an integral part of Greek food culture, enhancing and complementing the flavors of the cuisine. Greek coffee, brewed slowly in a briki pot, is more than a drink—it is an experience, consumed leisurely and often accompanied by spirited conversation. Wine, cultivated in Greece for thousands of years, ranges from the crisp whites of Santorini to the robust reds of Nemea. Retsina, infused with pine resin, is a unique specialty with a distinct flavor that divides opinion but remains a cultural icon. Herbal teas, made from mountain herbs like sideritis, are prized for their health benefits and soothing qualities.

Dining in Greece is an act of hospitality, known as philoxenia, which translates to "friend to the stranger." This deeply ingrained cultural value ensures that guests are treated with warmth and generosity, whether they are family, friends, or visitors from afar. A typical Greek meal is a leisurely affair, beginning with meze and moving through multiple courses, all served family-style. Conversation flows freely, and the emphasis is on togetherness rather than formality. Even in the simplest taverna, the sense of being welcomed and cared for is palpable, making every meal a memorable experience.

Greek food culture is also defined by its adaptability and innovation. While it remains deeply rooted in tradition, it has evolved to incorporate influences from neighboring countries and modern culinary trends. Ingredients like cumin and cinnamon, introduced during centuries of trade and conquest, have become integral to many dishes. Contemporary Greek chefs are reimagining classic recipes, using techniques like molecular gastronomy to present familiar flavors in new and exciting ways. This fusion of old and new ensures that Greek cuisine remains dynamic and relevant, appealing to both purists and adventurous eaters.

The experience of Greek food extends beyond the plate to the markets, kitchens, and fields where it begins. Visiting a traditional laiki agora, or farmers' market, is a sensory delight, with stalls overflowing with vibrant produce, fragrant herbs, and freshly baked bread. In village kitchens, recipes are passed down through generations, each cook adding their personal touch to the family's culinary legacy. The olive groves, vineyards, and fishing boats that supply the ingredients are a testament to the labor and love that underpin every dish. Greek food culture is, at its core, a celebration of the connection between people, land, and tradition.

To partake in Greek food is to embrace a way of life that values simplicity, authenticity, and community. It is an invitation to slow down, to savor each bite, and to share in the joy of good company. Whether you are enjoying a home-cooked meal in a mountain village, sampling street food in a bustling city, or dining at a seaside taverna, the flavors of Greece leave an indelible mark. They speak of a culture that has endured the test of time, one that continues to find its expression in the act of gathering around the table. Greek food culture is a journey, not just through flavors but through the heart and soul of a nation.

Must-Try Dishes: Moussaka, Souvlaki, and Spanakopita

Moussaka, souvlaki, and spanakopita are three dishes that stand as proud representatives of Greek cuisine, each encapsulating the flavors, techniques, and traditions that define this rich culinary heritage. These iconic dishes, while distinct in their ingredients and preparation, share a common thread: they are rooted in simplicity yet elevated by the skill and care of the cook. Each one tells a story, not only of its origins but of the culture and people who have lovingly preserved it. For anyone venturing into Greek gastronomy, these dishes are essential stops on a journey through the country's culinary landscape, offering a taste of both its history and its vibrant present.

Moussaka is perhaps the most famous of Greek comfort foods, a layered casserole that combines eggplant, ground meat, and a luxurious béchamel sauce. Though its origins are debated, with variations found across the Balkans and the Middle East, moussaka as we know it today owes much to the culinary innovations of Nikolaos Tselementes, a Greek chef who modernized the dish in the 1920s. His version introduced the

French-inspired béchamel, a creamy sauce made from milk, butter, and flour, which forms the crowning layer of this hearty dish. The result is a harmonious blend of textures and flavors: the softness of roasted eggplant, the richness of spiced ground meat, and the silky smoothness of the béchamel, all bound together by the earthy undertones of cinnamon and nutmeg.

The preparation of moussaka is an art form, requiring both patience and attention to detail. It begins with the eggplants, which are sliced, salted, and left to drain to remove their natural bitterness. Once rinsed and patted dry, they are lightly fried or roasted until tender, a step that ensures they maintain their structure during baking. The meat sauce, traditionally made with lamb or beef, is simmered with onions, garlic, tomatoes, and a blend of warm spices, creating a deeply flavorful base. Assembly is a meticulous process, with layers of eggplant, meat sauce, and occasionally potatoes stacked in a baking dish before being topped with the béchamel. The dish is baked until golden and bubbling, filling the kitchen with an aroma that is both inviting and nostalgic. Slicing into a freshly baked moussaka reveals its distinct layers, each contributing to a dish that is as visually appealing as it is satisfying to eat.

Souvlaki, on the other hand, is a dish that embodies simplicity and portability, making it a favorite among locals and tourists alike. At its core, souvlaki consists of skewered and grilled meat, typically pork, chicken, or lamb, marinated in olive oil, lemon juice, garlic, and oregano. The marinade infuses the meat with a bright, herbaceous flavor while tenderizing it, ensuring that each bite is juicy and flavorful. Souvlaki is often served with accompaniments such as pita bread, tzatziki sauce, and a side of vegetables, creating a complete and satisfying meal.

What sets souvlaki apart is its versatility and accessibility. It is as much a street food staple as it is a backyard barbecue favorite, enjoyed by Greeks of all ages and backgrounds. In urban areas, souvlaki stands are a common sight, their grills sending up plumes of aromatic smoke that draw in passersby. Here, the dish is often served as a wrap, with the meat tucked into warm pita bread along with tomatoes, onions, and a dollop of tzatziki. This portable version is perfect for eating on the go, whether strolling through a market or exploring the ruins of an ancient temple. At home, souvlaki is an opportunity for families and friends to gather around the grill, sharing stories and laughter as the skewers sizzle.

The preparation of souvlaki is straightforward yet rewarding, making it an excellent dish for aspiring cooks to try their hand at. The key lies in the marinade, which should be allowed ample time to penetrate the meat, ideally overnight. Once skewered, the meat is grilled over high heat, with frequent turning to ensure even cooking and a slight char that enhances its flavor. The result is a dish that celebrates the natural taste of its ingredients, elevated by the smoky notes of the grill and the freshness of its accompaniments.

Spanakopita, a savory pie filled with spinach and feta cheese, is a testament to the Greek love of phyllo dough and the creativity it inspires. This dish, which can be found in bakeries, tavernas, and homes across Greece, is as versatile as it is delicious. It can be served as a snack, appetizer, or main course, its flaky layers and rich filling making it a crowd-pleaser at any time of day. Spanakopita's roots lie in the rural traditions of Greece, where farmers would use the greens and herbs available to them to create hearty and nourishing meals. Over time, the dish evolved to include feta cheese, adding a tangy creaminess that perfectly complements the earthy spinach.

The hallmark of a great spanakopita is its phyllo crust, which should be crisp and golden, shattering delicately with each bite. Achieving this requires a deft touch, as the paper-thin sheets of dough are notoriously fragile and prone to tearing. Each sheet is brushed with melted butter or olive oil before being layered into a baking dish, creating a buttery, flaky base for the filling. The filling itself is a vibrant mixture of spinach, feta, onions, and dill, bound together with eggs to give it structure. Once assembled, the pie is baked until the phyllo is deeply golden and the filling is set, its aroma filling the kitchen with the promise of something truly special.

Spanakopita's appeal lies not only in its flavor but in its adaptability. While the classic combination of spinach and feta is hard to beat, variations abound, with cooks incorporating ingredients such as leeks, herbs, or even other cheeses to suit their tastes. The dish can also be made in individual portions, with the filling wrapped in triangles of phyllo for a portable snack. Whether enjoyed warm from the oven or at room temperature, spanakopita is a dish that brings people together, its layers of flavor reflecting the care and tradition that go into its making.

Together, moussaka, souvlaki, and spanakopita represent the diversity and richness of Greek cuisine. Each dish has its own unique character, yet all share a commitment to using fresh, high-quality ingredients and showcasing them in ways that are both simple and sophisticated. They are more than just food—they are expressions of Greek culture, history, and hospitality. To taste these dishes is to experience a slice of Greece itself, a country where meals are not merely sustenance but celebrations of life, family, and tradition.

For those new to Greek cooking, these dishes offer an excellent starting point. They are approachable yet rewarding, allowing cooks to develop their skills while gaining a deeper appreciation for the techniques and flavors that define Greek cuisine. Whether it's the slow layering of moussaka, the rhythmic turning of souvlaki skewers on the grill, or the careful handling of fragile phyllo for spanakopita, each step is an opportunity to connect with the culinary traditions of Greece. By bringing these dishes to your table, you not only honor their heritage but also share in the joy and warmth that Greek food culture embodies.

Greek Desserts: Baklava, Loukoumades, and Beyond

Greek desserts are a reflection of the country's rich history, vibrant culture, and deep-rooted traditions. They are as much about the flavors as they are about the sense of occasion they create, a sweet finale to meals that often stretch into hours of conversation and laughter. From the crisp, layered indulgence of baklava to the golden, honey-drenched loukoumades, Greek sweets embody the Mediterranean ethos of simplicity elevated by technique and high-quality ingredients. These desserts are not only culinary masterpieces but also a connection to the past, with recipes that have been handed down through generations, ensuring that every bite carries with it the weight of tradition and the joy of celebration.

Baklava, perhaps the most famous Greek dessert, is a symphony of textures and flavors. This layered pastry, made with delicate sheets of phyllo dough, finely chopped nuts, and a sticky, aromatic syrup, is a marvel of culinary craftsmanship. Though its exact origins are debated, baklava has become synonymous with Greek desserts, treasured for its balance of sweetness, crunch, and spice. The preparation begins with the phyllo dough, a paper-thin pastry that requires patience and precision to handle. Each sheet is brushed with melted butter before being layered into a baking dish, forming the foundation of the dessert. Between these layers, a mixture of nuts—most commonly walnuts, almonds, or pistachios—is spread, often spiced with cinnamon or cloves for depth.

The assembly of baklava is meticulous, with the phyllo and nuts layered repeatedly until the dish is filled. Before baking, the pastry is carefully scored into diamond-shaped pieces, a step that ensures the syrup can seep evenly through the layers once it is added. The syrup, made from sugar, water, honey, and a hint of citrus or rosewater, is poured over the hot pastry as soon as it comes out of the oven. This allows the syrup to soak into the layers, imbuing the baklava with its characteristic sweetness and stickiness. The result is a dessert that is at once crisp and tender, its every bite an explosion of flavor. Baklava is often served during celebrations, from weddings to religious holidays, and its presence on the table signals a moment of indulgence and festivity.

Loukoumades, on the other hand, are a dessert that brings a sense of playfulness to the Greek culinary repertoire. These small, deep-fried dough balls, drizzled with honey and sprinkled with cinnamon or crushed nuts, are a favorite treat for both young and old. Loukoumades have a history that dates back to ancient Greece, where they were offered as prizes to victorious athletes during the Olympic Games. Today, they are enjoyed in homes, bakeries, and street markets, a testament to their timeless appeal. The dough for loukoumades is simple, made from flour, water, yeast, and a pinch of sugar, yet its transformation in hot oil is nothing short of magical.

The preparation of loukoumades involves dropping spoonfuls of the sticky dough into hot oil, where they puff up into golden orbs. The frying process requires a keen eye, as the dough must be cooked evenly to achieve its signature light and airy texture. Once removed from the oil, the loukoumades are immediately drizzled with warm honey, allowing the sweet syrup to cling to their crisp exterior. A sprinkling of cinnamon or a handful of chopped walnuts completes the dish, adding a layer of complexity to its flavor profile. Loukoumades are best enjoyed fresh and warm, their crispy outside giving way to a soft, pillowy center. They are often served during festivals, fairs, and family gatherings, their simplicity and charm making them a universal favorite.

Beyond baklava and loukoumades, Greek desserts encompass a wide range of flavors, textures, and techniques, each offering a unique insight into the country's culinary traditions. Galaktoboureko, for instance, is a custard-filled pastry that combines the crispness of phyllo with the creaminess of semolina-based custard. The custard, flavored with vanilla or orange zest, is encased in layers of buttered phyllo and baked until golden. Like baklava, galaktoboureko is soaked in a sugar syrup after baking, giving it a luscious, melt-in-the-mouth quality. This dessert is often served at special occasions, its rich, indulgent nature making it a centerpiece of any celebration.

Kourabiedes, almond shortbread cookies dusted generously with powdered sugar, are another staple of Greek dessert culture. These buttery treats are particularly popular during the Christmas season, their snowy appearance evoking the winter landscape. The dough, enriched with ground almonds and often scented with brandy or rosewater, is shaped into rounds or crescents before being baked to a delicate golden hue. Once cooled, the cookies are rolled in powdered sugar, creating a sweet coating that balances their nutty, buttery flavor. Kourabiedes are a symbol of hospitality and warmth, often offered to guests alongside a cup of coffee or tea.

Melomakarona, honey-dipped cookies flavored with orange and spices, are a seasonal favorite that rivals kourabiedes during the holidays. These oval-shaped cookies are made with a dough that incorporates olive oil, orange juice, and a hint of brandy, resulting in a tender, aromatic texture. After baking, the cookies are soaked in a honey syrup and sprinkled with crushed walnuts, creating a dessert that is both moist and fragrant. The combination of citrus, spice, and honey makes melomakarona a quintessentially Mediterranean treat, one that captures the essence of Greek holiday traditions.

Rice pudding, or rizogalo, offers a simpler yet deeply comforting dessert option. This creamy dish, made from rice, milk, sugar, and a touch of vanilla or cinnamon, is a staple in Greek households. Rizogalo is often served as an everyday treat, its gentle sweetness and smooth texture appealing to all ages. It is typically made with short-grain rice, which releases starch during cooking to create a thick, velvety consistency. Served warm or chilled, rizogalo is a reminder of the comforting role desserts play in Greek food culture, offering a sense of nourishment and care.

The use of honey, nuts, and spices in Greek desserts is a reflection of the country's agricultural bounty and its historical connections to the wider Mediterranean region. Honey, often referred to as "the nectar of the gods," has been a prized ingredient in Greek cuisine since antiquity, valued for its sweetness and medicinal properties. Nuts, including walnuts, almonds, and pistachios, are abundant in Greece and feature prominently in desserts, adding flavor, texture, and nutrition. Spices like cinnamon, cloves, and nutmeg, introduced through centuries of trade and conquest, lend warmth and complexity to many traditional sweets. These ingredients, combined with the skill of Greek cooks and pastry chefs, create desserts that are as rich in history as they are in flavor.

Greek desserts are more than just a conclusion to a meal; they are an expression of hospitality, tradition, and celebration. Whether enjoyed at a family gathering, a street festival, or a local bakery, these sweets bring people together, creating moments of joy and connection. They are a reminder of the simple pleasures in life, the way a crisp bite of baklava or the warmth of freshly fried loukoumades can brighten a day. For those exploring Greek cuisine, these desserts offer a taste of the country's soul, a sweet invitation to savor the richness of its culture and the warmth of its people.

Wine and Spirits: Ouzo, Retsina, and Greek Wines

Ouzo, retsina, and Greek wines are the lifeblood of Greece's drinking culture, each with its own distinct story and place in the country's history and way of life. These beverages are more than just drinks; they are symbols of Greek hospitality, tradition, and identity, deeply woven into the fabric of the nation. Whether sipped by the sea with a plate of meze, uncorked at a family celebration, or poured in a quiet moment of reflection, they offer a glimpse into the soul of Greece. Their flavors, steeped in the land and shaped by centuries of craftsmanship, speak of the country's rugged mountains, sun-drenched islands, and fertile plains. To understand ouzo, retsina, and Greek wines is to embark on a journey through the essence of Greek culture, where every sip tells a story.

Ouzo is perhaps the most iconic of Greek spirits, instantly recognizable by its distinctive anise flavor and its milky-white transformation when mixed with water. It is a drink that is as much about the experience as the taste, a ritual that brings people together in moments of joy, conversation, and companionship. Its production is a testament to the artistry of Greek distillers, who blend high-quality alcohol with anise and other botanicals such as fennel, mastiha, or cinnamon to create a spirit that is both aromatic and complex. The exact recipes are often closely guarded secrets, passed down through generations of distillers who take pride in their craft.

The proper way to enjoy ouzo is a topic of much discussion among Greeks, but certain traditions hold true. It is typically served in small glasses, accompanied by a carafe of cold water and a selection of meze—small plates of food that might include olives, feta, grilled octopus, or fried zucchini. The addition of water or ice transforms the clear spirit into a cloudy emulsion, a phenomenon known as the "ouzo effect," which occurs when the essential oils in the anise become insoluble. This ritual of diluting ouzo not only enhances its flavor but also encourages slow sipping, making it a drink to be savored rather than rushed. Ouzo is rarely consumed without food, as its strong flavor and high alcohol content are best balanced by the salty, savory, and tangy notes of traditional Greek meze.

While ouzo is often associated with leisurely afternoons at seaside tavernas, it also has a role in more formal settings and celebrations. It is a drink that bridges the gap between casual and ceremonial, equally at home in a bustling market as at a wedding or baptism. Its versatility is part of its charm, as is its ability to evoke a sense of place. To sip ouzo is to be transported to Greece, to feel the warmth of the sun on your skin and hear the gentle lapping of the waves against the shore.

Retsina is another uniquely Greek offering, a wine that has been infused with pine resin to create a flavor profile unlike any other. Its origins date back thousands of years, to a time when wine was stored in amphorae sealed with resin to prevent spoilage. While the use of resin as a preservative became obsolete with the advent of modern winemaking techniques, the distinctive taste it imparted to the wine remained popular, evolving into the retsina we know today. This golden-hued wine is often misunderstood by those unfamiliar with it, as its piney aroma and slightly resinous taste can be an acquired taste. However, for many Greeks, it is a beloved staple, a nostalgic link to the country's ancient winemaking traditions.

Retsina is best enjoyed with food, as its bold flavors pair particularly well with the earthy, herbaceous, and tangy notes of Greek cuisine. Dishes like grilled fish, stuffed grape leaves, or spanakopita are natural companions, their flavors harmonizing with the wine's unique character. Served chilled, retsina is refreshing and invigorating, its crisp acidity cutting through rich or oily dishes with ease. For those new to retsina, it is worth seeking out high-quality examples from producers who take care to balance the resin's influence with the natural flavors of the wine. Modern winemakers have embraced retsina's heritage while refining its production, creating wines that are both traditional and approachable.

Greek wines, too, have a story to tell, one that stretches back to antiquity. Greece is one of the world's oldest wine-producing regions, with a history that predates the Roman Empire and even the rise of classical Athens. The ancient Greeks revered wine as a gift from Dionysus, the god of wine and revelry, and their winemaking techniques laid the foundation for the wine cultures of Europe. Today, Greece boasts a diverse range of wines, each shaped by the country's varied climates, soils, and indigenous grape varieties. From the volcanic slopes of Santorini to the rolling hills of Nemea, Greek vineyards produce wines that are as distinctive as the landscapes they come from.

One of the most celebrated Greek wines is Assyrtiko, a white wine that thrives on the island of Santorini. Grown in volcanic soil and shaped by the island's harsh winds and intense sunlight, Assyrtiko is known for its crisp acidity, minerality, and citrus flavors. It is a wine that pairs beautifully with seafood, its bracing freshness cutting through the richness of dishes like grilled octopus or lemon-drizzled fish. Santorini's unique basket-shaped vines, trained close to the ground to protect them from the elements, are a testament to the ingenuity and resilience of Greek winemakers.

Another standout is Agiorgitiko, a red wine grape native to the Nemea region of the Peloponnese. Often referred to as the "blood of Hercules," Agiorgitiko produces wines that range from light and fruity to rich and full-bodied, depending on how the grapes are cultivated and vinified. Its versatility makes it a favorite among winemakers and wine lovers alike, with flavors of red fruit, spice, and a hint of earthiness that make it a natural pairing for roasted meats, tomato-based dishes, and aged cheeses.

Xinomavro, another prominent red grape, is grown primarily in the northern regions of Greece, such as Naoussa and Amyndeon. Known for its high acidity and tannins, Xinomavro is often compared to Nebbiolo, the grape behind Italy's Barolo. Its complex flavors of dark fruit, olives, and dried herbs make it a wine that rewards aging, with older vintages developing notes of leather, tobacco, and truffle.

Xinomavro is a wine for contemplation, its layers of flavor unfolding slowly and rewarding those who take the time to savor it.

The diversity of Greek wines extends far beyond these examples, with a wealth of indigenous grape varieties waiting to be discovered. Whites like Moschofilero and Malagousia offer floral and aromatic profiles, while reds like Limniona and Mandilaria showcase the wealth of flavors that Greek terroirs can produce. Dessert wines, too, are a highlight of Greek winemaking, with the sweet, sun-dried wines of Samos and the luscious Vinsanto of Santorini standing out as exceptional examples.

The culture of wine and spirits in Greece is inseparable from the concept of philoxenia, the Greek tradition of hospitality. To share a glass of ouzo, retsina, or wine is to extend a hand of friendship, to invite someone into your world and celebrate the moment together. These drinks are not merely beverages; they are rituals, expressions of gratitude and connection that transcend language and borders. In Greece, drinking is rarely done in isolation; it is a communal act, a way of bringing people together and celebrating life's simple pleasures.

Ouzo, retsina, and Greek wines are more than just staples of Greek drinking culture—they are symbols of the country's history, its generosity, and its enduring connection to the land. They are drinks that demand to be experienced, not just tasted, each one offering a unique perspective on what it means to be Greek. Whether you are raising a glass at a bustling taverna, toasting at a family gathering, or sipping quietly by the sea, these beverages invite you to slow down, to savor the moment, and to connect with something greater than yourself. They are, in every sense, Greece in a glass.

The Art of the Greek Coffee and Meze Culture

Greek coffee and meze culture are two pillars of Greek social life, offering more than just sustenance—they are rituals that bring people together, strengthen bonds, and celebrate the art of living. From the preparation of a rich, aromatic cup of coffee to the vibrant array of small dishes shared among friends, these traditions are deeply embedded in Greek identity. They are not rushed experiences but deliberate acts of connection, where time slows down, and the focus shifts to savoring flavors, sharing stories, and enjoying the present moment. Together, they represent the essence of Greek hospitality, encapsulating the warmth and generosity for which the country is renowned.

Greek coffee, known as "ellinikós kafés," is more than just a beverage; it is a cultural symbol and a cherished daily ritual. Its roots can be traced back centuries, influenced by Ottoman coffee traditions, yet over time, it has evolved into something distinctly Greek. Prepared in a small, long-handled pot called a "briki," Greek coffee is made with finely ground coffee beans, cold water, and, if desired, sugar. The briki is placed over low heat, and as the coffee slowly warms, it forms a thick foam called "kaimaki" on the surface—a sign of a well-prepared cup. Achieving the perfect kaimaki requires patience and skill, as the coffee must be heated gently to avoid boiling, which would disrupt the foam and alter the flavor.

The preparation process itself is an almost meditative act. The briki is carefully watched, and as the coffee begins to rise, it is removed from the heat just in time to preserve the kaimaki. Greek coffee is never stirred after it is poured into the small, handle-less cups in which it is traditionally served. The grounds settle at the bottom, creating a layer of sediment that is not consumed but often used for fortune-telling in informal settings. The coffee is sipped slowly, its strong, earthy flavor complemented by the thick, smooth texture. It is not a drink meant for hurried consumption but one to be savored, preferably in the company of others.

The way Greek coffee is served and consumed reflects the country's emphasis on hospitality and connection. It is customary to offer coffee to guests as a gesture of welcome, often accompanied by a small sweet such as a piece of loukoumi (Turkish delight) or a spoon sweet made from preserved fruit. In traditional kafeneia, or coffeehouses, Greek coffee is the centerpiece of social interaction, enjoyed alongside animated discussions, card games, or simply the quiet act of people-watching. These spaces, found in nearly every village and neighborhood, are microcosms of Greek life, where locals gather to exchange news, debate politics, and nurture a sense of community.

Meze culture, like Greek coffee, is rooted in the idea of togetherness. The word "meze" originates from the Persian "mazzeh," meaning "taste" or "relish," and that is exactly what these small dishes are designed to do—offer a variety of tastes that complement drinks and encourage sharing. Meze is not a meal in the traditional sense but a social experience, often enjoyed with ouzo, tsipouro, or wine. The dishes are brought out gradually, creating a rhythm that allows the conversation to flow as freely as the drinks. There is no rush to finish; instead, the focus is on savoring each bite and relishing the company.

The variety of meze is staggering, reflecting the diversity of Greece's culinary traditions and its reliance on fresh, local ingredients. From the sea come grilled octopus, fried calamari, and marinated anchovies, each dish showcasing the simplicity and purity of Mediterranean flavors. Vegetables play a starring role in meze culture, with plates of roasted peppers, stuffed grape leaves (dolmades), and creamy dips like tzatziki (yogurt, cucumber, and garlic) and melitzanosalata (smoky eggplant spread). Cheese lovers will find plenty to enjoy, from saganaki, a pan-fried cheese served sizzling hot, to feta drizzled with olive oil and sprinkled with oregano. Meat-based meze includes spicy sausages like loukaniko, tender lamb kebabs, and meatballs (keftedes) seasoned with herbs and spices.

The presentation of meze is as important as the flavors themselves. The dishes are served on small plates, encouraging diners to sample a bit of everything and share with those around them. There is an inherent informality to the experience, a sense of spontaneity that makes every meze gathering unique. Whether enjoyed at a taverna by the sea or in someone's home, meze fosters a spirit of openness and conviviality. It is a way of dining that prioritizes connection over formality, where the act of sharing food becomes a celebration of relationships.

Greek coffee and meze culture are deeply intertwined, often enjoyed together as part of a leisurely afternoon or evening. A kafeneio might serve a simple meze platter alongside coffee, while a taverna will offer coffee as the final note to a long meal of shared dishes. Both traditions emphasize the importance of taking time to enjoy life's simple pleasures, a philosophy that is central to Greek culture. They are not about excess or indulgence but about creating moments of joy and connection in everyday life.

The role of these traditions extends beyond the table, influencing the way Greeks approach hospitality, friendship, and celebration. Offering coffee or meze is an act of generosity, a way of saying, "You are welcome here." It is a gesture that transcends language and cultural barriers, embodying the Greek concept of "philoxenia," or love for the stranger. This ethos is evident in the way guests are treated, whether they are lifelong friends or first-time visitors. In Greece, to share coffee or meze is to share a part of oneself, to invite others into a space of warmth and connection.

The rituals surrounding Greek coffee and meze are also a link to the past, preserving traditions that have been passed down through generations. The methods of preparing coffee, the recipes for dips and small plates, even the way the dishes are arranged on the table—all are rooted in history and memory. These traditions are a way of honoring the people and practices that came before, while also adapting to the present. Modern interpretations of meze, for example, might include new ingredients or techniques, but they remain true to the spirit of sharing and simplicity that defines the tradition.

At their core, Greek coffee and meze culture are about more than food and drink; they are about the act of coming together, of creating and cherishing connections. They teach us to slow down, to appreciate the moment, and to recognize the value of community. In a world that often feels rushed and fragmented, these traditions offer a reminder of what truly matters: the people we share our lives with and the simple pleasures that bring us joy. Whether you are sitting in a bustling kafeneio, gathered around a table laden with meze, or enjoying a quiet cup of coffee at home, you are participating in a tradition that is as timeless as it is meaningful. They are not just rituals but a way of life, a celebration of the art of living well.

CHAPTER 7: MODERN GREECE – VIBRANT CITIES AND CONTEMPORARY CULTURE

Thessaloniki: Greece's Cultural and Culinary Capital

Thessaloniki, Greece's second-largest city, is a vibrant mosaic of culture, history, and gastronomy that stands apart from the rest of the country. Situated in the heart of Macedonia, this northern city has long been a crossroads of civilizations, where East meets West, and the past intertwines seamlessly with the present. Its rich history, dynamic arts scene, and unparalleled culinary offerings make Thessaloniki a destination that embodies the spirit of modern Greece while honoring its deep historical roots. Known for its warm hospitality and youthful energy, Thessaloniki captivates visitors with its blend of ancient landmarks, bustling markets, and a food culture that rivals any in the Mediterranean.

The city's history is etched into every corner, from its Roman and Byzantine ruins to its Ottoman influences and Jewish heritage. Walking through Thessaloniki feels like peeling back layers of time. The Rotunda, originally built as a mausoleum for the Roman emperor Galerius, later transformed into a Christian church, then a mosque, and now a monument, is a testament to the city's complex past. Nearby, the Arch of Galerius, adorned with intricate carvings depicting the emperor's victories, serves as a gateway to the city's Roman heart. Thessaloniki's Byzantine legacy is just as prominent, with its many UNESCO-listed churches like Hagios Demetrios and Hagia Sophia showcasing stunning mosaics and architectural grandeur. These sacred spaces offer a glimpse into the city's role as a major center of Christianity during the Byzantine Empire.

The White Tower, Thessaloniki's most iconic landmark, stands proudly on the city's waterfront, a reminder of its Ottoman era. Once a prison and now a museum, the White Tower offers panoramic views of the Thermaic Gulf and the city's sprawling urban landscape. Nearby, the Ladadika district, once a hub for olive oil traders, has been transformed into a lively area filled with tavernas, bars, and vibrant street art. The juxtaposition of old and new is striking—Thessaloniki is a city that wears its history proudly while embracing the cosmopolitan energy of the present.

Thessaloniki's Jewish history is another integral part of its identity. For centuries, the city was home to a thriving Sephardic Jewish community, earning it the nickname "Mother of Israel." The Monastir Synagogue, the Jewish Museum of Thessaloniki, and the Holocaust Memorial stand as reminders of this once-flourishing community and the tragic events of World War II. Today, efforts to preserve and honor Thessaloniki's Jewish heritage are evident throughout the city, adding another layer to its rich cultural tapestry.

What sets Thessaloniki apart from other Greek cities is its youthful vibrancy. As a university town with a large student population, the city buzzes with creative energy and innovation. The streets are alive with festivals, concerts, and exhibitions, reflecting a dynamic arts scene that embraces both tradition and modernity. The Thessaloniki International Film Festival, held annually, attracts filmmakers and cinephiles from around the globe, while the city's many galleries and cultural centers showcase contemporary Greek art alongside historical treasures. Music is also a cornerstone of Thessaloniki's cultural life, with venues offering everything from traditional rebetiko to cutting-edge electronic beats.

At the heart of Thessaloniki's charm is its culinary scene, which melds flavors from its diverse cultural influences into a gastronomic paradise. The city's location at the crossroads of trade routes has brought together Greek, Ottoman, Jewish, and Balkan culinary traditions, creating a food culture that is as unique as it is delicious. Thessaloniki is known as Greece's culinary capital for a reason—every meal here is an opportunity to explore bold flavors, fresh ingredients, and time-honored recipes.

Start your culinary journey at one of Thessaloniki's bustling markets. Modiano Market, with its narrow alleys and vibrant stalls, is a feast for the senses. Here, vendors sell everything from freshly caught seafood to aromatic spices, while bakers pull trays of koulouri, the city's beloved sesame-covered bread rings, fresh from the oven. Nearby, Kapani Market offers a more traditional experience, with butchers, fishmongers, and grocers hawking their wares alongside stalls selling olives, cheese, and local wines. These markets are not just places to shop—they are windows into the daily lives of Thessaloniki's residents and a testament to the city's enduring connection to its food culture.

No visit to Thessaloniki is complete without sampling its famous bougatsa, a flaky pastry filled with sweet custard or savory fillings like cheese or minced meat. Served warm and dusted with powdered sugar or cinnamon for the sweet version, bougatsa is a beloved breakfast staple that locals swear by. Another must-try dish is soutzoukakia, spiced meatballs simmered in a rich tomato sauce, often served with rice or mashed potatoes. This dish, like so many others in Thessaloniki, reflects the city's Ottoman heritage, blending spices like cumin and cinnamon for a warming, deeply satisfying flavor.

Seafood lovers will find plenty to adore in Thessaloniki, where the proximity to the sea ensures a steady supply of fresh fish and shellfish. Head to a seaside taverna for grilled sardines, octopus marinated in vinegar, or a steaming bowl of kakavia, a traditional Greek fish soup. Pair your meal with a glass of ouzo or tsipouro, and let the flavors transport you to the heart of the Mediterranean. For a more casual experience, look for psarotavernes, small fish taverns that serve simple, perfectly cooked seafood dishes at reasonable prices.

Thessaloniki's sweets are as legendary as its savory dishes. Trigona panoramatos, triangular phyllo pastries filled with creamy custard and soaked in syrup, are a local specialty that epitomizes indulgence. Another favorite is tsoureki, a sweet, braided bread often flavored with mahleb or orange zest and sometimes filled with chocolate or chestnut cream. These treats, along with an array of baklava, galaktoboureko, and loukoumades, can be found in the city's patisseries, which are renowned for their artistry and attention to detail.

The city's café culture is another highlight, offering a chance to unwind and soak in Thessaloniki's relaxed atmosphere. Sidewalk cafés line the streets, serving everything from traditional Greek coffee to freddo cappuccinos, a chilled espresso drink that has become a local favorite. Take your coffee to Aristotelous Square, the city's grand central plaza, where you can sit and watch the world go by against a backdrop of neoclassical architecture and the shimmering sea.

Thessaloniki's neighborhoods each have their own distinct character, offering something for every traveler. Ano Poli, the city's old town, is a labyrinth of cobblestone streets, colorful houses, and hidden courtyards that feels like stepping back in time. The walls of the city's Byzantine fortifications offer sweeping views of Thessaloniki and the Thermaic Gulf, making it a favorite spot for photographers and romantics alike. In contrast, the city center buzzes with modern energy, its streets lined with shops, restaurants, and bars that stay open late into the night.

For those seeking a deeper connection to Thessaloniki's history, the city's museums are treasure troves of knowledge and artifacts. The Archaeological Museum of Thessaloniki houses an impressive collection of ancient Macedonian relics, including gold jewelry and funerary objects from the royal tombs of Vergina. The Museum of Byzantine Culture offers a fascinating look at the art, architecture, and daily life of the Byzantine era, while the State Museum of Contemporary Art showcases works by modern Greek and international artists.

Thessaloniki is more than just a city—it is an experience, a place that invites you to immerse yourself in its rhythms, flavors, and stories. From its ancient ruins to its bustling markets, from the aroma of freshly baked bread to the sound of rebetiko music spilling into the streets, Thessaloniki captures the essence of Greece in a way that is entirely its own. Whether you come for the history, the food, or the vibrant culture, you'll leave with a piece of this city in your heart, eager to return and uncover even more of its treasures.

Patras: A Blend of History and Festivities

Patras, a coastal city nestled in the northern Peloponnese, is a vibrant tapestry of history, culture, and unrelenting festivity. As Greece's third-largest city and a major port connecting the country to Western Europe, Patras has long been a gateway to the Mediterranean, a crossroads where ancient legacies and modern traditions converge. Known for its lively spirit and world-renowned carnival, Patras offers a unique blend of historical depth and exuberant celebration, making it a destination that captivates the heart and soul of its visitors. From its fascinating archaeological sites to its pulsating modern energy, the city is a shining example of Greece's ability to honor its past while embracing the present.

The roots of Patras stretch back thousands of years, and its history is intertwined with myth and legend. According to ancient Greek mythology, the city was founded by Patreus, the leader of the Achaeans, after he united three neighboring settlements. Archaeological evidence suggests that the area has been inhabited since the Neolithic period, and it played a significant role during the Mycenaean era. Later, under

Roman rule, Patras flourished as a cosmopolitan hub, known for its trade, culture, and impressive architecture. The remains of this Roman legacy can still be seen today, offering a glimpse into the city's storied past.

One of the most striking remnants of Roman influence is the Odeon of Patras, an ancient theater that dates back to the 1st century AD. This well-preserved structure, located in the upper part of the city, once hosted performances and public gatherings in antiquity. Today, it continues to serve as a cultural venue, hosting concerts and theatrical productions that bring the stones of history to life. Nearby, the Roman Amphitheater and the ruins of the Roman aqueduct further illustrate the city's importance during this era, providing a tangible connection to a time when Patras was a thriving center of commerce and art.

The medieval period brought its own transformations to Patras, as the city became a contested stronghold during the Byzantine Empire and later under Frankish, Venetian, and Ottoman rule. The Castle of Patras, perched on a hill overlooking the city, is a testament to this turbulent era. Built in the 6th century on the ruins of an ancient acropolis, the fortress offers panoramic views of the Gulf of Patras and the surrounding landscape. Its walls, towers, and gates tell the story of a city that has stood resilient in the face of centuries of conflict and change.

As you wander through the streets of Patras, the layers of history become ever more apparent. The city's architectural landscape is a fascinating blend of neoclassical mansions, modern structures, and remnants of its Byzantine and

Ottoman past. The Apollon Theatre, designed by Ernst Ziller in the 19th century, stands as a jewel of neoclassical elegance in the heart of the city. This iconic building, located in Georgiou I Square, serves as a cultural hub and a reminder of Patras' role as a beacon of the arts during Greece's modern history.

Yet, it is not just history that defines Patras—it is the city's boundless energy and love for celebration. Patras Carnival, known as "Patrino Karnavali," is the largest and most famous carnival in Greece, drawing thousands of visitors from across the country and beyond. With roots dating back to the Venetian era, the carnival has evolved into a spectacular extravaganza of parades, costumes, music, and dance. The festivities begin in January and culminate on the weekend before Clean Monday, marking the start of Lent in the Orthodox calendar.

The Grand Parade, the highlight of the carnival, is a dazzling display of creativity and exuberance. Floats adorned with elaborate designs, costumed participants dancing to infectious rhythms, and confetti raining down from the skies create an atmosphere of pure joy. The city transforms into a colorful playground, where locals and visitors alike come together to revel in the spirit of celebration. Another cherished tradition of the Patras Carnival is the Treasure Hunt, a game that involves solving riddles, completing challenges, and exploring the city in search of clues. This interactive event brings people of all ages together, fostering a sense of camaraderie and adventure.

Patras' festive spirit extends beyond the carnival season. Throughout the year, the city hosts a variety of cultural events, festivals, and exhibitions that reflect its dynamic personality. The International Film Festival of Patras, for instance, showcases emerging talent in filmmaking, while the Wine Festival celebrates the region's rich viticultural heritage. Music lovers can enjoy performances ranging from classical concerts to contemporary gigs, often held in open-air venues that take advantage of the city's stunning coastal scenery.

No visit to Patras would be complete without indulging in its culinary delights. The city's gastronomy is a reflection of its diverse history and fertile surroundings, offering a rich array of flavors that delight the palate. Fresh seafood is a highlight of the local cuisine, with dishes like grilled octopus, fried calamari, and saganaki shrimp taking center stage. The fertile plains surrounding Patras produce an abundance of fruits, vegetables, and olives, which find their way into traditional recipes like briam (roasted vegetables) and horta (wild greens).

Patras is also known for its sweet treats, particularly its famous loukoumades—golden, honey-drenched doughnuts that are a staple of Greek dessert culture. Another local specialty is pasteli, a sesame and honey bar that has been enjoyed since ancient times. These simple yet satisfying treats are perfect accompaniments to a cup of Greek coffee, best enjoyed at one of the city's many cafés.

Wine has played a central role in Patras' identity for centuries, and the region is home to some of Greece's most celebrated vineyards. The Achaia region, where Patras is located, produces a variety of wines that showcase the diversity of Greek viticulture. Mavrodaphne, a sweet red wine with a deep, complex flavor, is a local specialty that has gained international acclaim. Another notable wine is Roditis, a crisp and aromatic white wine that pairs beautifully with the city's seafood dishes. Many wineries in the area offer tours and tastings, providing visitors with the opportunity to learn about the winemaking process and sample the fruits of the region's labor.

For those seeking a deeper connection to nature, the surrounding region of Patras offers a wealth of outdoor activities and natural beauty. The Gulf of Patras, with its sparkling waters and gentle breezes, is ideal for sailing, windsurfing, and fishing. Inland, the lush hills and mountains provide opportunities for hiking, mountain biking, and exploring traditional villages that seem untouched by time. The Rio-Antirrio Bridge, an architectural marvel that connects the Peloponnese to mainland Greece, is a striking sight and a symbol of modern engineering excellence.

Patras is a city that invites exploration, discovery, and celebration. Whether you are delving into its ancient past, joining in the exuberance of its carnival, savoring its culinary treasures, or simply strolling along its sun-drenched promenade, Patras offers an experience that is as multifaceted as it is unforgettable. It is a place where history and festivity coexist in harmony, where every corner holds a story waiting to be told, and where the warmth of its people makes you feel instantly at home. To visit Patras is to embrace the joy of life, to celebrate the beauty of the present while honoring the echoes of the past.

Volos: Gateway to the Mythical Pelion

Volos, a picturesque port city nestled at the foot of Mount Pelion, is a place where myth and reality intertwine seamlessly. As the gateway to the mythical Pelion peninsula, Volos holds a special place in Greek culture, history, and geography, offering visitors a unique blend of urban charm and access to some of the most breathtaking landscapes in Greece. Known as the home of Jason and the Argonauts, who set sail aboard the Argo in their quest for the Golden Fleece, Volos is steeped in ancient legend. Yet, it is also a thriving modern city, brimming with life, culinary delights, and a rich maritime heritage. Its strategic location, vibrant spirit, and proximity to the enchanting villages and forests of Pelion make it an essential stop for anyone seeking to explore the magic of Greece.

The city's waterfront is the heart of Volos, a lively promenade that stretches along the Pagasetic Gulf, offering stunning views of the sea and the docked fishing boats swaying gently in the breeze. Cafés, bars, and restaurants line the promenade, their terraces filled with locals and visitors enjoying the relaxed atmosphere. It's a place where time seems to slow down, where conversations are unhurried, and where the sound of the waves provides a soothing backdrop to the rhythm of daily life. As the sun sets over the gulf, the waterfront comes alive with a warm golden glow, drawing people together to share in the simple pleasures of the moment.

Volos has a long and storied history that dates back to the Neolithic period, making it one of the oldest continuously inhabited areas in Greece. Archaeological sites such as Dimini and Sesklo, located just outside the city, reveal the remnants of some of Europe's earliest settlements. These sites offer a fascinating glimpse into the lives of the region's ancient inhabitants, with their intricately designed pottery, advanced urban planning, and evidence of early trade networks. The Archaeological Museum of Volos houses many of the artifacts unearthed from these sites, including tools, ornaments, and ceremonial objects, providing visitors with a deeper understanding of the area's prehistoric heritage.

The city's connection to mythology is most famously tied to Jason and the Argonauts. According to legend, Volos was the starting point of their epic journey, and the modern city embraces this mythological heritage with pride. A replica of the Argo, painstakingly constructed using traditional shipbuilding techniques, is docked at the port, serving as a symbol of the city's maritime past and its ties to the ancient world. Visitors can admire the craftsmanship of this vessel and imagine the daring voyage it represents—a story of adventure, courage, and the pursuit of the unknown.

What sets Volos apart from other Greek cities is its unique culinary tradition, centered around the art of the tsipouro meze. Tsipouro, a strong distilled spirit similar to ouzo, is the star of Volos' dining scene, and the city is dotted with tsipouradika—traditional taverns where this drink is served alongside an array of small plates, or meze. Each round of tsipouro is accompanied by a different selection of meze, ranging from grilled octopus and fried anchovies to stuffed peppers and creamy dips. The variety and quality of these dishes reflect the region's abundant natural resources and culinary creativity. Sharing tsipouro and meze with friends or family is more than a meal; it's a ritual of connection, laughter, and celebration that captures the essence of Greek hospitality.

Volos is also a gateway to the enchanting Pelion peninsula, a region steeped in natural beauty and mythological significance. In Greek mythology, Pelion was the home of the Centaurs, the half-human, half-horse beings known for their wisdom and wild nature. It was also the site of the wedding of Peleus and Thetis, the parents of Achilles, where the infamous golden apple of discord led to the events that sparked the Trojan War. Today, Pelion remains a place of wonder, where lush forests, crystal-clear waters, and charming villages create a landscape that feels almost otherworldly.

The villages of Pelion are among its greatest treasures, each with its own character and charm. Makrinitsa, often called the "balcony of Pelion," is a stunning village perched on the mountainside, offering panoramic views of Volos and the Pagasetic Gulf. Its cobblestone streets, stone-built mansions, and traditional fountains transport visitors to another time, while its vibrant squares buzz with the energy of locals and travelers alike. Just a short distance away, Portaria combines the tranquility of nature with a lively cultural scene, making it a popular destination for both relaxation and exploration.

Pelion's natural beauty is unparalleled, with its dense forests of chestnut, beech, and plane trees providing a cool respite from the summer heat. Hiking trails crisscross the peninsula, leading adventurers through verdant valleys, past gurgling streams, and up to breathtaking vistas. The Centaur's Path, a trail near Portaria, is particularly enchanting, winding through a forested ravine that feels straight out of a fairy tale. For those seeking a more leisurely experience, the scenic Pelion Train, also known as the Moutzouris, offers a nostalgic journey through the countryside, passing over stone bridges and through picturesque villages.

The beaches of Pelion are another highlight, with their turquoise waters and pristine sands offering a perfect escape from the hustle and bustle of daily life. On the Aegean side, beaches like Mylopotamos and Fakistra are known for their dramatic cliffs and crystal-clear waters, while the calmer shores of the Pagasetic Gulf, such as Kala Nera and Afissos, provide a more tranquil setting. Each beach has its own unique character, from hidden coves accessible only by boat to lively stretches of sand lined with beach bars and tavernas.

The seasons in Pelion bring their own unique charm, making it a year-round destination. In the spring, the hillsides burst into bloom, with wildflowers carpeting the meadows and the scent of herbs filling the air. Summer brings long, sunny days perfect for swimming, hiking, and exploring the villages. Autumn transforms the forests into a tapestry of red, orange, and gold, creating a magical atmosphere that is ideal for photography and outdoor activities. Winter, meanwhile, turns Pelion into a snowy wonderland, with the ski resort at Chania offering opportunities for skiing and snowboarding against the backdrop of the Aegean Sea.

Volos and Pelion together offer a harmonious blend of urban sophistication and natural splendor, making them a destination that appeals to a wide range of travelers. Whether you're drawn to the city's vibrant waterfront, its rich history, or its exceptional food culture, or whether you're seeking the tranquility and adventure of Pelion's landscapes, this region has something to offer everyone. It's a place where myths come to life, where every corner holds a story waiting to be discovered, and where the warmth of its people makes you feel instantly at home.

Greece's Emerging Art and Music Scene

The creative pulse of Greece has always beat in rhythm with its storied history, but today, a new wave of artists and musicians is redefining the cultural landscape, making Greece a vibrant hub for contemporary art and music. Far from being confined to its ancient monuments and classical traditions, the nation's creative energy is bursting forth in workshops, galleries, music venues, and public spaces. Whether through provocative street art in urban Athens, dynamic performances in Thessaloniki, or experimental music festivals on the islands, Greece's emerging art and music scene is carving out a space that balances its rich heritage with an innovative, forward-thinking identity.

Athens, the country's capital, is at the epicenter of this artistic renaissance. While its ancient ruins dominate the skyline, the streets below tell a different story. The neighborhoods of

Exarchia, Psirri, and Metaxourgio have become canvases for some of Europe's most compelling street art. Walls that were once bare now explode with color and political commentary, telling stories of economic hardship, resilience, and hope. Internationally acclaimed street artists such as INO and STMTS have left their mark here, creating large-scale murals that are as thought-provoking as they are visually striking. It's not uncommon to stumble upon pieces that grapple with themes like social justice, migration, or identity, turning the streets into an open-air gallery that evolves by the day.

Beyond its street art, Athens is home to a burgeoning gallery scene that showcases both established and emerging talent. The Benaki Museum, known for its collection of historical artifacts, has expanded its scope to include contemporary art exhibitions. Meanwhile, smaller spaces like the Breeder Gallery and the National Museum of Contemporary Art (EMST) have become essential stops for those seeking cutting-edge works. These galleries provide a platform for Greek artists to experiment with mediums ranging from installation and video art to performance and sculpture. The result is a thriving community of creators who are unafraid to push boundaries and challenge conventions.

Thessaloniki, often regarded as Greece's cultural capital, is another hotspot for contemporary art and music. The city's dynamic energy is palpable, fueled by its large student population and international influences. The Thessaloniki Biennale of Contemporary Art has established itself as a major event on the global art calendar, drawing artists and audiences from around the world. Each edition of the Biennale explores a different theme, often addressing pressing social and political issues through a Mediterranean lens. The city's art scene extends far beyond the Biennale, with spaces like MOMus (Metropolitan Organization of Museums of Visual Arts) fostering creativity and dialogue year-round.

Music is equally central to Greece's cultural evolution, with a new generation of musicians reshaping the country's soundscape. Athens has emerged as a melting pot of genres, where rebetiko—Greece's traditional urban folk music—intersects with electronica, hip-hop, and jazz. Venues such as Gazarte and Six d.o.g.s serve as incubators for experimental sounds, hosting performances that range from intimate acoustic sets to high-energy DJ nights. Greek artists like Sofia Kourtesis and Sillyboy's Ghost Relatives have gained international recognition for their innovative approaches, blending local influences with global trends to create music that feels both rooted and boundaryless.

Thessaloniki's music scene is equally vibrant, with a particular emphasis on live performances. The city's waterfront venues and underground clubs buzz with activity, offering everything from indie rock to traditional Balkan rhythms. Reworks Festival, an annual celebration of electronic music and digital art, has become a cornerstone of Thessaloniki's cultural calendar. The festival attracts world-renowned DJs and producers while also spotlighting local talent, creating a space where the global and the local collide in perfect harmony.

The islands of Greece, long celebrated for their natural beauty, are also playing a role in the country's cultural renaissance. Syros, for example, has become a surprising hub for contemporary music and art. The island hosts the Animasyros

International Animation Festival, which brings together filmmakers and animators from across the globe. Meanwhile, the Syros International Film Festival offers a platform for experimental cinema, often incorporating live performances and site-specific installations into its programming. These events showcase the island's ability to merge its idyllic setting with a forward-thinking artistic vision.

Crete, too, has embraced the intersection of tradition and innovation. The island's music scene is deeply rooted in its history, with the lyra—a pear-shaped, three-stringed instrument—serving as a symbol of its cultural identity. At the same time, contemporary musicians are reinterpreting these traditional sounds, infusing them with modern elements to create something entirely new. Festivals like Houdetsi, held in a small village outside Heraklion, celebrate this fusion, drawing audiences who are eager to experience Crete's evolving musical language.

One of the most exciting developments in Greece's cultural scene is the rise of interdisciplinary festivals that blur the lines between art, music, and technology. Athens Digital Arts Festival (ADAF) is a prime example, showcasing works that integrate virtual reality, interactive installations, and multimedia storytelling. The festival transforms urban spaces into playgrounds of creativity, inviting audiences to engage with art in ways that are immersive and participatory. Similarly, ADD Festival, dedicated to electronic music and digital art, has become a platform for boundary-pushing performances that challenge traditional notions of what music and art can be.

Public spaces across Greece are also being transformed into stages for creative expression. The Stavros Niarchos Foundation Cultural Center in Athens, with its state-of-the-art facilities and sprawling park, hosts free concerts, film screenings, and art exhibitions that are open to all. Similarly, the Technopolis complex, housed in a former gasworks, has become a hub for cultural events, from jazz festivals to art fairs. These venues represent a broader movement toward democratizing culture, making it accessible to a wider audience and fostering a sense of community through shared experiences.

The economic challenges of recent years have played a paradoxical role in fueling Greece's creative explosion. Artists and musicians, often operating with limited resources, have found innovative ways to collaborate and share their work. DIY spaces, pop-up galleries, and grassroots initiatives have flourished, driven by a spirit of resilience and resourcefulness. This sense of collective creativity has not only enriched Greece's cultural landscape but has also positioned it as a hub for emerging talent on the international stage.

What makes Greece's emerging art and music scene particularly compelling is its ability to balance tradition and modernity. Whether it's a street artist drawing inspiration from Byzantine iconography, a musician reimagining rebetiko with electronic beats, or a filmmaker exploring ancient myths through a contemporary lens, Greek creators are constantly finding new ways to honor their heritage while breaking new ground. This duality—rooted yet forward-looking—is what gives Greece's cultural renaissance its unique character.

For those visiting Greece, engaging with its art and music scene offers a deeper understanding of the country's identity. Beyond the archaeological sites and postcard-perfect landscapes, there is a vibrant, dynamic culture that reflects the complexities and contradictions of modern Greece. Whether you're exploring a gallery in Athens, dancing at a music festival in Thessaloniki, or discovering an experimental film on an island, you'll find that Greece's creative spirit is as inspiring as its ancient ruins.

This renaissance is a testament to the enduring power of creativity to transform, connect, and rejuvenate. In a country that has long been synonymous with history, Greece's emerging art and music scene serves as a reminder that its story is far from over. It is a story being written in vivid colors and bold sounds, one that invites everyone to take part in its ongoing evolution.

Shopping in Greece: Local Crafts, Jewelry, and Souvenirs

Shopping in Greece is a journey that takes you far beyond bustling markets and charming boutiques; it's an exploration of the country's rich traditions, craftsmanship, and artistic heritage. From intricate jewelry inspired by ancient designs to handcrafted ceramics, embroidered textiles, and unique culinary products, Greece offers a treasure trove of items that embody the spirit of its land and people. Every purchase has a story to tell, rooted in centuries of history and passed down through generations of artisans. Whether you're exploring the winding streets of Athens, the vibrant markets of Thessaloniki, or the quaint villages of the islands, Greece provides endless opportunities for finding meaningful souvenirs that go far beyond the ordinary.

Athens, the capital and cultural heart of Greece, is an essential starting point for discovering the country's diverse offerings. The Monastiraki Flea Market, located in the heart of the city, is a lively maze of stalls and shops selling everything from handmade leather sandals to antique treasures. Here, you'll find skilled artisans crafting items that reflect Greece's identity while incorporating modern touches. A pair of leather sandals, for instance, is not just footwear but a nod to a tradition dating back to ancient times. Many shops offer customizable designs, allowing you to select the straps, colors, and embellishments that suit your style. These sandals are practical, durable, and steeped in history, making them a perfect keepsake or gift.

For jewelry enthusiasts, Greece is a paradise. The country's long-standing tradition of goldsmithing and silversmithing is evident in the exquisite pieces available in cities and villages alike. Athens' Plaka district is home to numerous jewelers whose collections often feature motifs inspired by ancient Greek art and mythology. Look for necklaces adorned with the meander pattern, symbolizing infinity, or earrings shaped like olive branches, a nod to Athena, the goddess of wisdom. Beyond Athens, the island of Rhodes is renowned for its intricate filigree work, while Ioannina in Epirus is famed for its silver craftsmanship. Whether you choose a simple pendant or an elaborate bracelet, each piece carries a connection to Greece's artistic legacy.

Venturing into Thessaloniki, you'll discover a city that blends tradition with contemporary flair. The city's Kapani Market is a sensory feast, filled with stalls offering everything from spices and herbs to handcrafted soaps and textiles. Thessaloniki's creative scene also extends to its boutiques, where young designers reinterpret traditional Greek aesthetics in clothing, accessories, and home decor. These modern takes on heritage crafts make for unique purchases that are both stylish and meaningful. Additionally, the city is known for its vibrant ceramic art, with many workshops producing hand-painted plates, bowls, and tiles that capture the colors and patterns of the region.

The islands of Greece each have their own distinct character, reflected in their artisanal products. Crete, for example, is celebrated for its woven textiles, pottery, and leather goods. The village of Anogeia, set high in the mountains, is particularly famous for its handwoven rugs and blankets, created using techniques that have remained unchanged for generations. These pieces, often adorned with geometric patterns and vibrant colors, are not just decorative but also deeply symbolic, representing the island's cultural heritage. Pottery is another highlight of Crete, with workshops in villages like Margarites offering a chance to see artisans at work, shaping and painting each piece with meticulous care.

Santorini, renowned for its dramatic landscapes, also has a thriving arts and crafts scene. The island's volcanic soil lends itself to the production of unique ceramic goods, often inspired by the natural beauty and rich history of the area. From vases and plates to figurines and jewelry, Santorini's ceramics make for stunning keepsakes. Additionally, the island is known for its handmade jewelry, with many shops offering pieces that incorporate semi-precious stones, sea glass, and lava beads. These materials, sourced locally, add a distinctive touch to each creation, making them a true reflection of the island's essence.

On the island of Corfu, the Venetian influence is evident in its local crafts. Kumquat liqueur, made from the small citrus fruit introduced to the island during Venetian rule, is a must-try and a perfect souvenir. The liqueur is often sold in decorative bottles shaped like Greek amphorae, adding an artistic flair to this culinary delight. Corfu is also known for its handmade lace and embroidery, which can be found in villages like Lefkimmi and Kassiopi. These delicate textiles, often featuring intricate floral patterns, are a testament to the skill and patience of the island's artisans.

Beyond crafts and jewelry, Greece offers a wealth of edible souvenirs that capture the flavors of the Mediterranean. Olive oil, often referred to as liquid gold, is one of the country's most prized exports. Greek olive oil is renowned for its quality and taste, with varieties from regions like Kalamata and Crete being particularly sought after. Many producers offer artisanal oils infused with herbs, citrus, or truffle, providing a gourmet touch to an already exceptional product. Packaged in elegant bottles, they make for a practical yet luxurious gift.

Honey is another staple of Greek culinary heritage, with each region producing varieties that are distinct in flavor and aroma. Thyme honey from the islands, pine honey from the mountains, and chestnut honey from the forests each tell a story of the land they come from. Often sold in jars adorned with traditional motifs, Greek honey is not just a sweet treat but also a reflection of the country's biodiversity. Pair it with a package of loukoumi, the Greek version of Turkish delight, for a gift that combines taste and tradition.

Spices and herbs are also popular items to bring home, with oregano, thyme, and rosemary being staples of Greek cuisine. Saffron from the region of Kozani, known as Krokos Kozanis, is particularly prized for its vibrant color and distinct flavor. Packaged in small boxes or tins, these spices are both practical and evocative, allowing you to recreate the flavors of Greece in your own kitchen.

For those who appreciate traditional beverages, Greece offers a variety of options. Tsipouro and ouzo, both anise-flavored spirits, are quintessentially Greek and often sold in beautifully designed bottles. Mastiha, a liqueur made from the resin of the mastic tree found on the island of Chios, is another unique option. Its sweet, herbal flavor makes it a versatile drink, enjoyed as an aperitif or digestif. Greek wines, especially those from regions like Santorini, Nemea, and Naoussa, are also worth exploring, with many wineries offering bottles that are as visually striking as their contents are delicious.

Shopping in Greece is not just about the items themselves but also about the experiences that come with them. Visiting a workshop, watching an artisan at work, and learning about the history and significance of a craft add depth to each purchase. Many shops and markets encourage interaction, allowing you to ask questions, hear stories, and even try your hand at creating something yourself. These moments of connection transform a simple shopping trip into an opportunity to engage with Greece's culture on a personal level.

The act of bargaining, while not as common as it once was, still has a place in some markets, particularly in less touristy areas. Approach it with a sense of humor and respect, treating it as part of the cultural experience rather than a means to secure the lowest price. In many cases, the relationship you build with the vendor is just as valuable as the item you take home.

Every item you purchase in Greece carries with it a piece of the country's soul. Whether it's a handcrafted ceramic, a bottle of olive oil, or a piece of jewelry inspired by ancient designs, these treasures serve as lasting reminders of your journey. They tell stories of the people who made them, the land that inspired them, and the culture that sustains them. In a world where mass production often dominates, the handmade and the heartfelt stand out as symbols of authenticity and connection. Shopping in Greece is more than an activity—it's a way to take a piece of its magic home with you, ensuring that the memories of your travels remain vivid for years to come.

Greece's Nightlife: From Traditional Bouzoukia to Modern Clubs

Greece's nightlife is a vibrant tapestry woven with threads of tradition and modernity, lighting up the evenings with a unique blend of cultural richness and contemporary energy. Whether it's the haunting melodies of traditional live music at a bouzoukia, the pulsating rhythms of a beachside club, or the laid-back atmosphere of a seaside taverna, Greece offers a nightlife experience that caters to every taste. As the sun dips below the horizon and casts its golden glow over the Aegean or Ionian seas, the country comes alive in a way that is as intoxicating as it is unforgettable. From the heart of Athens to the islands' most secluded corners, Greek nightlife reflects the joy, passion, and community spirit of its people.

Athens, with its sprawling urban landscape and rich cultural heritage, sets the stage for some of the most diverse nightlife experiences in Greece. The city's neighborhoods each offer something distinctive, a reflection of Athens' multifaceted identity. In Psirri, a neighborhood where traditional meets trendy, small tavernas spill into cobblestone streets, their tables illuminated by the soft glow of lanterns. Live music fills the air, often performed by duos or trios playing rebetiko, a genre often referred to as the "Greek blues." These songs, infused with melancholy and longing, echo through the night, creating an atmosphere that feels timeless. Psirri is also home to a growing number of contemporary cocktail bars, where mixologists craft drinks inspired by Greek ingredients like mastiha, bergamot, and oregano.

In contrast, the upscale Kolonaki district caters to those seeking sophistication. Rooftop bars in this chic part of Athens offer panoramic views of the Acropolis, their sleek interiors lit up by the shimmering city below. These venues are perfect for sipping fine wines or indulging in innovative cocktails while enjoying the buzz of a cosmopolitan crowd. Meanwhile, Gazi, the city's former industrial area, has transformed into a hub of modern nightlife. The old gasworks have been repurposed into cultural spaces, and the surrounding neighborhood now boasts a mix of clubs, live music venues, and art spaces. Here, electronic beats dominate the scene, with DJs spinning until the early hours of the morning, drawing a diverse, international crowd.

The bouzoukia, however, remain the cornerstone of traditional Greek nightlife. These live music venues are a celebration of laiko, a genre of Greek popular music that has evolved over the decades but continues to resonate deeply with locals and visitors alike. Attending a bouzoukia is not merely a night out; it's an immersive cultural experience. The evening often begins with a meal of small meze dishes, accompanied by wine or ouzo. As the music starts, the energy in the room grows, with patrons clapping, singing along, and even throwing flowers at the performers—a gesture of admiration and respect. Major cities like Athens and Thessaloniki boast renowned bouzoukia establishments, often hosting famous singers who draw crowds eager to lose themselves in the music's emotional intensity.

Thessaloniki, Greece's cultural capital, also boasts a nightlife scene that rivals that of Athens. The city's waterfront is lined with bars and cafés that convert into lively spots as the evening progresses. Ladadika, a historic district near the port, is a favorite destination for both locals and tourists. Its narrow streets are filled with tavernas offering live music, from traditional Greek tunes to jazz and rock. Thessaloniki has a youthful energy, thanks in part to its large student population, and this vibrancy is reflected in its nightlife. Clubs and bars stay open until dawn, offering everything from techno and house music to alternative rock and hip-hop.

The islands, of course, are synonymous with Greece's legendary nightlife, each offering its own unique flavor. Mykonos, often referred to as the party capital of Greece, is a haven for those seeking high-octane nightlife. The island's beach clubs are world-famous, attracting international DJs and celebrities. Paradise Beach and Super Paradise Beach are the epicenters of this scene, where parties start in the afternoon and continue until the sun rises. The clubs here are renowned for their extravagant themes, cutting-edge sound systems, and unforgettable energy. Cavo Paradiso, perched on a cliff overlooking the sea, is one of the island's most iconic venues, offering an unparalleled experience of music, dance, and breathtaking views.

Santorini, while known for its romantic ambiance, also has a lively side that comes alive after dark. The island's capital, Fira, is home to a collection of bars and clubs that cater to a more eclectic crowd. Venues like Koo Club and Tango Bar offer a mix of open-air terraces and vibrant dance floors, where visitors can enjoy cocktails under the starlit Santorini sky. The island's nightlife, though less frenetic than Mykonos, is equally memorable, blending elegance with a festive spirit.

For a more relaxed and authentic experience, the islands of Paros and Naxos provide a charming alternative to the high-energy scenes of Mykonos and Santorini. Paros, with its laid-back vibe, is perfect for those who enjoy evenings spent at beach bars or quaint tavernas. Naoussa, a picturesque fishing village on the island, transforms into a nightlife hotspot after dark, with its harbor lined with bars offering everything from traditional Greek music to modern beats. Naxos, known for its family-friendly atmosphere, offers a quieter nightlife scene that focuses on community and culture. Small bars and cafés often feature live music performances, where locals mingle with visitors in a warm, welcoming environment.

Crete, Greece's largest island, offers a nightlife experience that is as diverse as its landscape. Heraklion, the island's capital, has a mix of traditional music venues and modern clubs, while Chania's old town is home to atmospheric bars and tavernas tucked away in narrow alleyways. Rethymno, with its Venetian harbor and fortress, provides a romantic setting for evenings spent sipping raki, the island's signature spirit. Crete's nightlife is deeply rooted in its traditions, with many venues featuring live performances of Cretan music, complete with lyra players and dancers in traditional costumes.

The smaller islands, often overlooked in favor of their more famous counterparts, also have their own unique nightlife scenes. In the Dodecanese, Rhodes combines medieval charm with a lively bar and club culture. The island's Old Town, a UNESCO World Heritage Site, is home to bars that make use of centuries-old buildings, creating an atmosphere that is both historic and modern. In the Cyclades, Milos offers a more intimate nightlife experience, with its small bars and seaside tavernas providing the perfect setting for relaxed evenings.

Greece's nightlife is not confined to its cities and islands; even its remote villages and mainland towns have their own ways of celebrating after dark. In the Peloponnese, traditional festivals known as panigyria are held throughout the summer, bringing communities together for nights of music, dancing, and feasting. These events are deeply rooted in local culture, often tied to religious celebrations, and offer visitors a chance to experience Greek hospitality at its most heartfelt.

What makes Greece's nightlife truly special is its diversity. It caters to every mood and preference, from the high-energy dance floors of Mykonos to the soulful melodies of a bouzoukia in Athens, from the chic rooftop bars of Thessaloniki to the quiet charm of a seaside taverna on Naxos. Each experience is a reflection of Greece's unique ability to balance tradition and modernity, creating nights that are as unforgettable as the days. Whether you're seeking excitement, romance, or a connection to the country's rich cultural heritage, Greece's nightlife offers it all, lighting up the night in ways that are both magical and deeply human.

CHAPTER 8: FINAL THOUGHTS AND REFLECTIONS

Reflecting on Greece's Magic

Greece is a land unlike any other, where every corner brims with a unique kind of enchantment that seems to transcend time itself. It is a place where ancient ruins whisper secrets of civilizations long gone, where the turquoise waters of the Aegean shimmer under the golden sun, and where the scent of wild herbs mingles with salty sea breezes. Yet, the magic of Greece goes far beyond its physical beauty. It is found in its rhythm of life, its deep-rooted traditions, and the warmth of its people. Greece is not merely a destination—it is a feeling, a state of being, a place that lingers in the heart long after one's journey ends.

Walking through Greece is like stepping into a living history book. The past and present coexist here in ways that feel almost surreal. In Athens, the Acropolis rises high above the city, its marble columns glowing in the sunlight, a symbol of human ingenuity and resilience. As you wander through its grounds, it is impossible not to imagine the philosophers, poets, and statesmen who once walked the same paths, shaping ideas that continue to influence the world today. Yet, just below, the city buzzes with modern energy—cafes filled with laughter, bustling markets, and street musicians playing melodies that carry the soul of Greece. This juxtaposition of antiquity and modernity is one of Greece's most captivating qualities, a reminder that the past is never far away.

Beyond the cities, Greece's landscape unfolds in a stunning array of contrasts. The islands, each with its own character, feel like jewels scattered across the Aegean and Ionian Seas. On Santorini, whitewashed buildings cling to cliffs that plunge dramatically into the caldera, their bright facades contrasting with the deep blue of the sea. Mykonos, with its labyrinthine streets and iconic windmills, exudes a cosmopolitan charm, while Crete, the largest of the islands, offers rugged mountains, ancient Minoan ruins, and a cuisine that is the very definition of farm-to-table. Every island tells its own story, yet all share the same warm hospitality and unhurried pace that invite visitors to forget the rush of modern life.

The mainland, too, holds treasures that reveal Greece's multifaceted magic. The towering peaks of Mount Olympus, once believed to be the home of the gods, inspire awe with their rugged beauty and mythological significance. In Meteora, monasteries perch precariously atop towering rock formations, their serene interiors a striking contrast to the dramatic landscape that surrounds them. In the Peloponnese, ancient sites like Epidaurus and Mycenae transport visitors to a time when myths were woven into the fabric of daily life. And then there is Delphi, the navel of the ancient world, where the oracle once spoke in cryptic riddles that shaped the destinies of kings and empires. Standing there, surrounded by mountains and olive groves, it is easy to understand why the ancients believed this was a place touched by the divine.

Greece's magic is not confined to its landmarks—it is also in its traditions and the way they are lovingly preserved. The country's calendar is filled with festivals and celebrations that bring communities together, blending religious devotion with sheer joy. Easter in Greece is an experience like no other, a week of rituals and feasts that culminates in the midnight Resurrection service, where candles are lit, and the words "Christos Anesti" fill the air. In the summer, village squares come alive with panigiria, traditional festivals featuring music, dancing, and endless plates of food. These events are more than just celebrations; they are expressions of Greece's soul, a way of honoring the past while embracing the present.

Food is central to Greece's identity, and it is here that the country's magic truly shines. A meal in Greece is not just about sustenance—it is a celebration of life, a moment to connect with others and savor the gifts of the land and sea. From the simplicity of a village salad, with its ripe tomatoes, crisp cucumbers, and briny feta, to the complex layers of moussaka or the delicate sweetness of baklava, every dish tells a story. The flavors of Greece are rooted in its geography and history, shaped by the sun, the sea, and the hands of those who have tended its fields and vineyards for generations. To share a meal in Greece is to experience its generosity, to feel the deep connection between the land and its people.

Perhaps the most magical aspect of Greece is its people. There is a warmth and openness here that is immediately disarming, a genuine hospitality that makes strangers feel like family. Whether it is a fisherman offering a fresh catch, a shopkeeper sharing a story, or a taverna owner insisting you try their homemade wine, the people of Greece are as much a part of its magic as its landscapes and history. They embody the concept of philoxenia, the love of strangers, a value that has been passed down through generations. It is this spirit of openness and generosity that makes Greece feel like home, no matter how far you have traveled to get there.

Greece is also a land of contrasts, where the sacred and the everyday coexist in perfect harmony. In the same breath, you can light a candle in a centuries-old church and join a group of locals in a lively dance. You can hike through a pristine gorge in the morning and sip ouzo by the sea as the sun sets. This ability to embrace life in all its forms is what makes Greece so special. It is a place where joy and reverence go hand in hand, where every moment is an opportunity to celebrate the beauty of existence.

The magic of Greece has a way of staying with you, long after you have left its shores. It lingers in the taste of olive oil, the sound of a bouzouki, the memory of a sunset that seemed to stretch across eternity. It is a place that invites you to slow down, to appreciate the simple pleasures of life, and to find beauty in the everyday. Greece is not just a country—it is an experience, a feeling, a reminder of what it means to be alive. To visit Greece is to be forever changed, to carry a piece of its magic with you wherever you go.

Share Your Experience: Tips for Future Travelers

Traveling to Greece is an experience that leaves an indelible mark on those who visit, but more than the awe of ancient ruins or the beauty of its azure waters, it's the small details, the moments that resonate deeply, that create lasting memories. For future travelers, the best advice is to embrace Greece not as just another destination but as a way of life. The country rewards those who are curious, open, and willing to step off the beaten path. While landmarks like the Acropolis, Santorini's caldera, or Delphi's oracle may be on every itinerary—and rightly so—there's so much more to discover if you know how to approach your journey. Here are some essential tips to help you make the most of your time in Greece, drawn from countless travelers' experiences who have fallen in love with this enchanting land.

Begin your journey with flexibility in mind. Greece is not a country that adheres strictly to schedules or timetables, and neither should you. Ferries can be delayed, restaurants may open later than expected, and a casual stroll through a village might lead to an impromptu invitation to join a local celebration. These moments of spontaneity are where the real magic happens, so it's worth building some extra time into your plans. If you're hopping between islands, leave room for the unforeseen—a chance encounter, a recommendation from a local, or simply the desire to linger a little longer in a place that speaks to your soul. Rigid itineraries can detract from Greece's charm, which thrives on the unhurried rhythm of its days.

Packing for Greece is an art in itself, and it begins with understanding the country's climate and terrain. Lightweight, breathable clothing is essential for navigating the hot, sunny days, especially during summer when temperatures can soar. Comfortable walking shoes are a must, as cobblestone streets and uneven pathways are common in both cities and villages. Layers are helpful for cooler evenings, especially in the spring and autumn months, when the weather can be unpredictable. Don't forget essentials like sunscreen, a wide-brimmed hat, and sunglasses to protect yourself from the Mediterranean sun, which can be surprisingly intense even in early spring. If you plan to visit churches or monasteries, pack a scarf or shawl to cover your shoulders, as modest dress is often required.

Learning a few basic Greek phrases can go a long way in enhancing your experience. While many Greeks speak English, especially in tourist areas, making an effort to greet someone with a friendly "Kalimera" (good morning) or "Efharisto" (thank you) is always appreciated. The Greek language is an integral part of the country's identity, and showing respect for it can open doors—both literally and figuratively. Locals are often delighted when visitors attempt to speak their language, no matter how clumsy the pronunciation might be, and this small gesture can lead to more authentic interactions.

When it comes to dining, take your time. Greek meals are not rushed affairs but opportunities to connect with others and savor the bounty of the land and sea. Seek out family-run tavernas away from the main tourist hubs, where the food is often prepared with love and care, using recipes that have been passed down for generations. Don't hesitate to ask the server for recommendations or to inquire about the day's specials—many dishes are made fresh daily and may not appear on the menu. Expand your palate by trying local specialties, from grilled octopus to gemista (stuffed vegetables) and from avgolemono soup to the lesser-known cheeses of each region. Meals in Greece are communal experiences, and sharing dishes with your companions is part of the tradition, so order a variety of plates to sample as much as possible.

Transportation in Greece can be its own adventure, and understanding how to navigate it will make your trip smoother. While renting a car is often the best way to explore the mainland, especially remote areas like Pelion or the Mani Peninsula, driving in Greece can be challenging for the uninitiated. Roads are often narrow and winding, and local drivers have a reputation for being assertive. On the islands, scooters and ATVs are popular options, but they require caution, as roads can be steep and traffic unpredictable. Public transportation, including buses and ferries, is generally reliable, though schedules may change without notice. If you're traveling between islands, consider the type of ferry you book—fast ferries are quicker but can be more expensive and less stable in rough seas, while traditional ferries are slower but offer an authentic experience with stunning views.

While Greece's iconic destinations are undoubtedly worth a visit, don't overlook its lesser-known gems. Islands like Naxos, Syros, and Amorgos offer a quieter, more authentic experience compared to the bustling hotspots of Mykonos and Santorini. On the mainland, regions like Epirus, Zagorohoria, and Thessaly provide breathtaking natural beauty, from dramatic gorges to pristine mountain lakes. These places often have fewer tourists, allowing for a deeper connection to the land and its people. Even within popular locations, there are hidden corners to discover—an unmarked trail that leads to a secluded beach, a small café where the owner still serves customers personally, or a local market bursting with color and life.

Respect for local customs and traditions is crucial when traveling in Greece. This is a country with a deep sense of history and pride in its culture, and honoring that will enrich your experience. Dress modestly when visiting religious sites, and always ask permission before taking photographs, particularly of people. Be mindful of the environment, especially on the islands, where resources like water are scarce. Avoid single-use plastics whenever possible, and support local businesses by purchasing handmade crafts, regional wines, or olive oils. These small acts demonstrate an appreciation for Greece's heritage and help sustain its communities.

Timing your visit can make a significant difference in your experience. While summer is the most popular time to visit, spring and autumn offer their own unique charms. In April and May, the countryside is lush with wildflowers, and the weather is warm but not overwhelming. September and October bring fewer crowds and a gentler heat, with the added bonus of harvest festivals and wine tastings. Winter, though quieter, has its own appeal, particularly for those interested in exploring Greece's cultural heritage without the throngs of tourists. Sites like Delphi, Meteora, and Athens take on a serene quality in the cooler months, and the snow-capped peaks of the mainland offer opportunities for hiking and even skiing.

One of the most valuable lessons for any traveler to Greece is to embrace the concept of *meraki*. This untranslatable word embodies the idea of pouring your heart and soul into what you do, whether it's cooking a meal, crafting a piece of art, or simply enjoying a moment. In Greece, you'll find *meraki* in the way a grandmother tends her garden, in the care a fisherman takes to mend his nets, and in the joyful chaos of a village festival. As a traveler, adopting this mindset will help you appreciate the beauty in the details and the joy in the simplest of moments.

Traveling in Greece is as much about the connections you make as it is about the sights you see. Take the time to talk to locals, whether it's a shopkeeper in a bustling market, a fisherman mending nets by the harbor, or a shepherd tending his flock in the hills. These interactions often lead to unexpected insights, stories, and even invitations that can transform your trip. Greeks are known for their hospitality, and many are eager to share their favorite spots, recipes, or anecdotes with visitors. These connections are what turn a good trip into an unforgettable one, reminding you that travel is ultimately about the people you meet along the way.

Greece is a country that rewards those who approach it with curiosity, respect, and an open heart. It is a place where the past and present coexist in harmony, where every meal is a celebration, and where the smallest moments—watching the sunset over the Aegean, sipping coffee in a quiet square, or hearing the laughter of children playing in the streets—can leave the deepest impressions. For future travelers, the greatest advice is this: don't just visit Greece—let it embrace you. Slow down, take it all in, and allow yourself to be transformed by its magic. After all, Greece is not just a destination; it's an experience that stays with you long after you've left its shores.

BONUS 1: ESSENTIAL PHRASES FOR YOUR DAILY TRAVEL NEEDS IN GREECE

BONUS 2: PRINTABLE TRAVEL JOURNAL

BONUS 3: 10 TIPS "THAT CAN SAVE THE DAY" ON YOUR TRIP IN GREECE

Made in the USA
Las Vegas, NV
31 March 2025